Making Disciples, Making Leaders
Participant Workbook

SECOND EDITION

Making Disciples, Making Leaders

Participant Workbook

SECOND EDITION

A Manual for Presbyterian Church Leader Development

Steven P. Eason
E. Von Clemans

Geneva Press
Louisville, Kentucky

Book design by Sharon Adams
Cover design by Allison Taylor

♾ The paper used in this publication meets the minimum requirements of the American National Standard for Information Sciences—Permanence of Paper for Printed Library Materials, ANSI Z39.48-1992.

*We are grateful to the ruling elders and deacons
with whom we have had the pleasure of serving in ordered ministry.
Their corrections, suggestions, and feedback over the years have
refined this leadership development model into the useful tool it is today.
They have shown us again and again when you ask for a lot, you get a lot.
Their willingness to respond to God's call and their effectiveness
as spiritual leaders in the Church proves the effort needed
to develop spiritual leaders is worth it. It has been a team effort,
and we as pastors and the Church have benefited.
We dedicate this book to all of you with deep appreciation.*

Contents

Supplemental Resources—43

Introduction

We have found if you raise the bar, people will jump higher! If you don't expect much, you won't get much. So we ramped up the training of our deacons and ruling elders. The result has been a much stronger leadership team within the church. What we discovered was that most churches were providing little or no training. The training provided was focused solely on the *Book of Order* or learning the rules. Most folks were not satisfied with the results.

Our focus is on *formation* rather than mere *information*. We see this as a time to build a team. It's a time for you to grow in your faith. It's a time to deepen your discipleship. So the training is ongoing. It's more than just knowing the rules. It goes past the budget, buildings, programs, and staff. It's not about church maintenance. It's about Christian leadership.

We invite you to see this as a time to go to the next level. There's something in here for you. At the end of your three-year term we anticipate that you will be a different person. Your church will be a different church. Not because you know more, but because you have shifted from "running a church" to "deepening your discipleship" in Christ. That's exciting.

There is a lot of work to do. Time management will be essential. Prayer needs to intensify. You may need to sacrifice something else in order to get this done. It's that important.

You are called and ordained to ordained ministry in the church. That's some serious business. You are on a team with the clergy in your church. It matters what happens here. The church needs leadership. Leadership needs to be empowered to lead. All leaders are first called to be disciples.

Do all the assignments. Read all of the books. Come to all of the meetings. Throw yourself into this as your service is to Christ himself. He has thrown himself into it for all of us.

Preparation

Books You Will Need

1. A Bible: All Scripture passages used in this *Participant Workbook* are from the New Revised Standard Version (NRSV). You may want to speak with your leaders about other translations or paraphrases that can be used.
2. *Making Disciples, Making Leaders Workbook,* 2nd ed. Louisville, KY: Geneva Press, 2015. (This text)
3. *Selected to Serve: A Guide for Church Leaders*, 2nd ed. Louisville, KY: Geneva Press, 2012.
4. *Book of Confessions,* Office of the General Assembly, Louisville, KY: Presbyterian Distribution Services, 2007.
5. *Book of Order 2013–2015,* Office of the General Assembly, Louisville, KY: Presbyterian Distribution Services, 2013.

NOTE: If the PC(USA) Constitution changes in the coming years, you will need to make the appropriate changes to any references used in this *Participant Workbook*. Please also note that the numbered parenthetical citations used throughout the book refer to the *Book of Order*.

Pre-Class Survey

Name: _____ Date: _____

Your responses to this survey will be compiled anonymously.
Please include your name so we can track who has completed the survey.

Topic	Rating
1. As you prepare for ordination/installation, to what extent do you feel prepared to assume your ministry? **1**=not prepared <==> **5**=very prepared	
Comments: _____ _____	
2. We are all at different places on our journey of faith and readiness to serve as a leader in ordered ministry. For each specific area listed, rate your sense of preparedness before beginning this training process. **1**=not prepared <==> **5**=very prepared	
My personal faith	
My knowledge of PC(USA) doctrine	
My knowledge of PC(USA) governance	
My knowledge of PC(USA) discipline	
My understanding of the duties of ruling elders and deacons	
My readiness as a spiritual leader	
Comments: _____ _____ _____	
3. At the beginning of this training course, how would you assess your current enthusiasm for serving as ruling elder or deacon? **1**=very apprehensive <==> **5**=very enthusiastic	
Comments: _____ _____	

Leader Development Overview and Assignments

"The session shall provide a period of study and preparation, after which the session shall examine them as to their personal faith; knowledge of the doctrine, government, and discipline contained in the Constitution of the church; and the duties of the ministry. The session shall also confer with them as to their willingness to undertake the ministry appropriate to the order." (G-2.0402)

Workshop 3h:15m	Worship 30 min.	Part 1 45 min.	Meal 30 min.	Part 2 45 min.	Small Groups 45 min.	Assignments (To be done prior to the class.)
#1	Worship 1	**Personal Faith** Your Faith Journey and Call to Serve (a) Constitutional Questions a–i (overview) [see W-4.4003 (a)–(i)]				☐ Book of Order: preface ☐ Book of Confessions: preface, part iii, pp. xx–xxix ☐ **Selected to Serve**: Chapters 1, 7 ☐ Participant Workbook (PW): Study Guide Section 1 (1.1–1.6) ☐ Worksheet: My Fears and Concerns ☐ Worksheet: My Faith Journey ☐ Worksheet: Constitutional Questions
#2	Worship 2	**Doctrine and Theology** What Presbyterians Believe (c) The Bible and Essential Tenets (b, d)				☐ Book of Order: F-1, 2 ☐ Book of Confessions: prefaces to each confession ☐ **Selected to Serve**: Chapter 6 ☐ PW: Study Guide Section 2 (2.1–2.15) ☐ Worksheet: To Be or Not to Be—Reformed! ☐ Worksheet: *Book of Confessions* chart ☐ Worksheet: To Be a Christian
#3	Worship 3	**Governance, Worship, and Discipline** The Presbyterian Way (e, f, g, h) When Things Go Wrong (e)				☐ Book of Order: F-3; G-1, 2.01–0105, 3, 6; W-1, 2, 5; D-1, 2 ☐ Book of Confessions: Confession of 1967 ☐ **Selected to Serve**: Chapters 3, 4, 5, 8 ☐ PW: Study Guide Sections 3, 4, 5 ☐ Worksheet: Presbyterian Principles ☐ Worksheet: Worship True/False Quiz ☐ Worksheet: Case Study #1: Maintaining the Purity of the Church
#4	Worship 4	**The Work of Ministry** What Ruling Elders/Deacons Do (i) How This Church Works				☐ Book of Order: G-2.01–2.04 ☐ Book of Confessions: A Brief Statement of Faith ☐ **Selected to Serve**: Chapter 9 ☐ PW: Study Guide Section 6 (6.1–6.9); review questions 3.5, 3.6 ☐ Worksheet: Duties of Ordered Ministries ☐ Worksheet: Writing Your Statement of Faith ☐ Worksheet: (opt.) Writing Your Financial Stewardship Journey

Preparation Study Guide for Exam

The session shall provide a period of study and preparation, after which the session shall examine them as to their personal faith; knowledge of the doctrine, government, and discipline contained in the Constitution of the church; and the duties of the ministry. The session shall also confer with them as to their willingness to undertake the ministry appropriate to the order. (G-2.0402)

In addition to your other assignments (see *Overview and Assignments Chart*), these questions will help you prepare for the examination by the session at the end of your training process. At that examination, examiners may choose from among the questions found here. Each of the four workshops will address questions from different sections of this Study Guide.

Most of the questions in sections 2–5 can be answered by judicious use of the indexes in the *Book of Order* and the *Book of Confessions*. Make note of the constitutional references as you research the questions. If you need additional space to write your answers, please do so on additional pieces of paper.

1. Personal Faith (no right or wrong answers)

1.1 What is the story (outline) of how you came to be a person of faith?

_____

_____

_____

_____

_____

_____

1.2 What people have been influential in the development of your faith? In what ways?

_____

_____

_____

_____

_____

_____

1.3. Over the course of your life, what are some of the things that have increased your faith? What has challenged your faith?

_____

_____

_____

1.4. What are some of the factors that went into your decision to accept the call to be a church leader?

_____

_____

_____

_____

1.5. Which constitutional question is the most challenging for you? (See W-4.4003.) Why?

_____

_____

_____

1.6. [*REQUIRED QUESTION*] What, if any, of the ordination questions can you not, in good conscience, answer in the affirmative? Why?

_____

_____

_____

_____

2. Knowledge of Doctrine

2.1. Who is the head of the Presbyterian Church (U.S.A.)?

_____

2.2. What does it mean to say "God alone is Lord of the conscience"?

_____

_____

_____

2.3. Which of the Great Ends of the Church has the highest priority for you? Why?

_____

_____

_____

_____

2.4. What is a confession?

_____

_____

_____

2.5. Why are confessions important in our tradition?

_____

_____

_____

2.6. Why do we have more than one confession?

_____

_____

_____

2.7. How many confessions are in the *Book of Confessions*?

_____

2.8. What is the purpose of the *Book of Confessions*?

_____

_____

_____

2.9. Which two confessions are shared by all Christians worldwide (the Church catholic)?

_____

_____

2.10. Which confessions were formed in the 20th century, and what were their particular historical contexts?

_____

_____

_____

_____

_____

_____

2.11. What are some *watchwords* of the Protestant Reformation?

_____

_____

_____

2.12. What is the *central affirmation* of the Reformed Tradition?

_____

_____

_____

2.13. Name one other affirmation of the Reformed Tradition

_____

2.14. Name one element the church is called to as the body of Christ.

_____

_____

_____

2.15. Why does the Presbyterian Church (U.S.A.) have such a strong emphasis on diversity and inclusiveness?

_____

_____

_____

_____

3. Knowledge of Government

3.1. What documents make up the Constitution of the Presbyterian Church (U.S.A.)?

_____

_____

_____

3.2. What are the parts of the *Book of Order,* and what is each part's special focus?

_____

_____

_____

_____

_____

3.3. Name one of the Principles of Presbyterian Government.

_____

_____

_____

3.4. What are the three ordained ministries in the Presbyterian Church?

_____

_____

_____

3.5. What are the duties and responsibilities of ruling elders and sessions?

_____

_____

_____

_____

_____

3.6. What are the duties and responsibilities of deacons and the Board of Deacons?

_____

_____

_____

_____

_____

3.7. Name the four councils in the Presbyterian system and briefly describe their function(s).

_____

_____

_____

_____

_____

3.8. How do you understand this statement from the *Book of Order*: "Presbyters are not simply to reflect the will of the people, but rather to seek together to find and represent the will of Christ"? (F-3.0204)

_____

_____

_____

_____

4. Knowledge of Worship and Sacraments

4.1. Name the six elements of Christian worship.

_____

_____

_____

4.2. What is the typical order of service in Presbyterian worship?

_____

_____

_____

_____

4.3. What part does Scripture play in our worship and life together?

_____

_____

_____

4.4. What is the primary role of music and musicians in worship?

_____

_____

4.5. Name the sacraments that are celebrated in the Presbyterian Church (U.S.A.).

_____

4.6. What are the biblical roots of each of the sacraments?

_____

_____

4.7. What is the significance (meaning) of each of the sacraments?

_____

_____

_____

_____

4.8. What are some of the ways our worship service integrates Scripture, proclamation, prayer, and praise?

_____

_____

_____

5. Knowledge of Discipline

5.1. What is the purpose of church discipline?

_____

_____

_____

5.2. What are the two types of judicial cases?

_____

5.3. What is the difference between a dissent and a protest?

_____

_____

_____

6. Knowledge of This Congregation

(These answers are not in your assigned readings; research on your own.)
6.1. When was this church founded? How old is it now?

_____

6.2. How many pastors have served this congregation?

_____

6.3. How many ruling elders and deacons (and trustees) do we have?

_____

6.4. Who is the current clerk of session?

_____

6.5. Who is the current moderator/chair of the Board of Deacons?

_____

6.6. [If your church has trustees] Who is the current chair/moderator of the Trustees?

_____

6.7. What are the major committees (councils, ministries, workgroups, etc.) of the session?

_____

_____

_____

6.8. What are the major committees (councils, ministries, workgroups, etc.) of the Board of Deacons?

_____

_____

_____

6.9. Does this church have a mission statement? If so, what is it?

_____

_____

_____

Constitutional Questions for Ordination, Installation, and Commissioning

In Workshop 1, you will have an opportunity to respond to the following constitutional questions (see W-4.4003).

The moderator of the council of those to be ordained, installed, or commissioned shall ask them to stand before the body of membership and to answer the following questions:

a. Do you trust in Jesus Christ your Savior, acknowledge him Lord of all and Head of the Church, and through him believe in one God, Father, Son, and Holy Spirit?

b. Do you accept the Scriptures of the Old and New Testaments to be, by the Holy Spirit, the unique and authoritative witness to Jesus Christ in the Church universal, and God's Word to you?

c. Do you sincerely receive and adopt the essential tenets of the Reformed faith as expressed in the confessions of our church as authentic and reliable expositions of what Scripture leads us to believe and do, and will you be instructed and led by those confessions as you lead the people of God?

d. Will you fulfill your ministry in obedience to Jesus Christ, under the authority of Scripture, and be continually guided by our confessions?

e. Will you be governed by our church's polity, and will you abide by its discipline? Will you be a friend among your colleagues in ministry, working with them, subject to the ordering of God's Word and Spirit?

f. Will you in your own life seek to follow the Lord Jesus Christ, love your neighbors, and work for the reconciliation of the world?

g. Do you promise to further the peace, unity, and purity of the church?

h. Will you pray for and seek to serve the people with energy, intelligence, imagination, and love?

i. (1) (For ruling elder) Will you be a faithful ruling elder, watching over the people, providing for their worship, nurture, and service? Will you share in government and discipline, serving in councils of the church, and in your ministry will you try to show the love and justice of Jesus Christ?

(2) (For deacon) Will you be a faithful deacon, teaching charity, urging concern, and directing the people's help to the friendless and those in need, and in your ministry will you try to show the love and justice of Jesus Christ?

(3) (For teaching elder) Will you be a faithful teaching elder, proclaiming the good news in Word and Sacrament, teaching faith and caring for people? Will you be active in government and discipline, serving in the councils of the church; and in your ministry will you try to show the love and justice of Jesus Christ?

(4) (For ruling elder commissioned to particular pastoral service) Will you be a faithful ruling elder in this commission, serving the people by proclaiming the good news, teaching faith and caring for the people, and in your ministry will you try to show the love and justice of Jesus Christ?

(5) (For certified Christian educator) Will you be a faithful certified Christian educator, teaching faith and caring for people, and will you in your ministry try to show the love and justice of Jesus Christ?

My Fears and Concerns

In the Bible, when God calls leaders into specific ministry, leaders often respond with surprise, fear, and reluctance. What fears and concerns do you bring as you begin leader training?

Please use a sheet of paper to record your answer. Bring it with you to the first worship service. Print or write legibly. Your anonymous responses will be mixed in with other leader-elects' responses and read out loud as part of the prayer of confession at worship.

Personal Faith

Your Faith Journey and Call to Serve (W-4.4003 a)

Do you trust in Jesus Christ your Savior, acknowledge him Lord of all and Head of the Church, and through him believe in one God, Father, Son, and Holy Spirit?

Constitutional Questions (W-4.4003 a–i)

Assignments

Book of Order: preface
Book of Confessions: preface, part iii, pp. xx–xxix
Selected to Serve: Chapters 1, 7
Participant Workbook: Study Guide Section 1 (1.1–1.6)
Worksheet: My Fears and Concerns
Worksheet: Constitutional Questions
Worksheet: My Faith Journey

Opening Worship

CALL TO WORSHIP

>   Leader: The Lord be with you.

>   **People: And also with you.**

PRAYER OF CONFESSION

>   Leader: We bring to God our fears and concerns

>   **All: (individual readings offered in random order)**

>   *Note: Participants are asked to write out their fears and concerns in taking office prior to the first session.*

ASSURANCE OF PARDON

>   Leader: In the name of Christ, we are forgiven.

>   **People: Thanks be to God! Amen.**

SCRIPTURE: Exodus 3:1–2, 9–15; 4:1–5, 10–17

Moses was keeping the flock of his father-in-law Jethro, the priest of Midian; he led his flock beyond the wilderness, and came to Horeb, the mountain of God. [2]There the angel of the LORD appeared to him in a flame of fire out of a bush; he looked, and the bush was blazing, yet it was not consumed. . . .

[9]"The cry of the Israelites has now come to me; I have also seen how the Egyptians oppress them. [10]So come, I will send you to Pharaoh to bring my people, the Israelites, out of Egypt." [11]But Moses said to God, "Who am I that I should go to Pharaoh, and bring the Israelites out of Egypt?" [12]He said, "I will be with you; and this shall be the sign for you that it is I who sent you: when you have brought the people out of Egypt, you shall worship God on this mountain."

[13]But Moses said to God, "If I come to the Israelites and say to them, 'The God of your ancestors has sent me to you,' and they ask me, 'What is his name?' what shall I say to them?" [14]God said to Moses, "I AM WHO I AM." He said further, "Thus you shall say to the Israelites, 'I AM has sent me to you.'" [15]God also said to Moses, "Thus you shall say to the Israelites, 'The LORD, the God of your ancestors, the God of Abraham, the God of Isaac, and the God of Jacob, has sent me to you':

This is my name forever,

and this my title for all generations. . . .

4 Then Moses answered, "But suppose they do not believe me or listen to me, but say, 'The LORD did not appear to you.'" [2]The LORD said to him, "What is that in your hand?" He said, "A staff." [3]And he said, "Throw it on the ground." So he threw the staff on the ground, and it became a snake; and Moses drew back from it. [4]Then the LORD said to Moses, "Reach out your hand, and seize it by the tail"—so he reached out his hand and grasped it, and it became

a staff in his hand—[5]"so that they may believe that the LORD, the God of their ancestors, the God of Abraham, the God of Isaac, and the God of Jacob, has appeared to you." . . . .

[10]But Moses said to the LORD, "O my Lord, I have never been eloquent, neither in the past nor even now that you have spoken to your servant; but I am slow of speech and slow of tongue." [11]Then the LORD said to him, "Who gives speech to mortals? Who makes them mute or deaf, seeing or blind? Is it not I, the LORD? [12]Now go, and I will be with your mouth and teach you what you are to speak." [13]But he said, "O my Lord, please send someone else." [14]Then the anger of the LORD was kindled against Moses and he said, "What of your brother Aaron, the Levite? I know that he can speak fluently; even now he is coming out to meet you, and when he sees you his heart will be glad. [15]You shall speak to him and put the words in his mouth; and I will be with your mouth and with his mouth, and will teach you what you shall do. [16]He indeed shall speak for you to the people; he shall serve as a mouth for you, and you shall serve as God for him. [17]Take in your hand this staff, with which you shall perform the signs."

REFLECTIONS

BIDDING PRAYERS

Response: Lord, hear our prayer.

COMMUNION

THE PEACE

Worksheet: My Faith Journey

Every faith/life journey is different. But everyone has a story. You are invited to share your story—to the extent you are comfortable—with others in your group.

The following chart may be helpful in telling your story. The horizontal scale indicates the years of your life. The vertical scale indicates your awareness (or lack of awareness) of God's presence in your life. You may want to mark significant life events on your timeline.

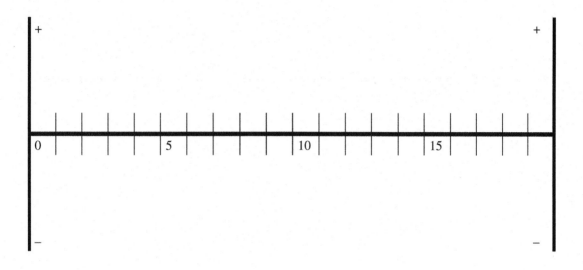

(continued on the next page)

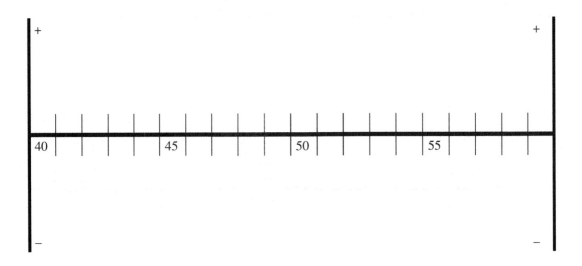

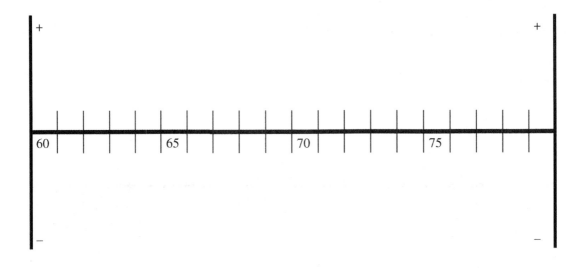

Worksheet: PC(USA) Constitutional Questions for Ordination, Installation, and Commissioning

Book of Order W-4.4003

Teaching elders, ruling elders, deacons, and educators—every person ordained in the Presbyterian Church (U.S.A.)—must answer affirmatively these questions.

Instructions

For each question, mark where you are right now using the following scale:

1=can't affirm **2**=some difficulty **3**=no enthusiasm or uncertain **4**=yes **5**=enthusiastic yes

#	Question
	a. Do you trust in Jesus Christ your Savior, acknowledge him Lord of all and Head of the Church, and through him believe in one God, Father, Son, and Holy Spirit?
	b. Do you accept the Scriptures of the Old and New Testaments to be, by the Holy Spirit, the unique and authoritative witness to Jesus Christ in the Church universal, and God's Word to you?
	c. Do you sincerely receive and adopt the essential tenets of the Reformed faith as expressed in the confessions of our church as authentic and reliable expositions of what Scripture leads us to believe and do, and will you be instructed and led by those confessions as you lead the people of God?
	d. Will you fulfill your **ministry** in obedience to Jesus Christ, under the authority of Scripture, and be continually guided by our confessions?
	e. Will you be governed by our church's polity, and will you abide by its discipline? Will you be a friend among your colleagues in ministry, working with them, subject to the ordering of God's Word and Spirit?
	f. Will you in your own life seek to follow the Lord Jesus Christ, love your neighbors, and work for the reconciliation of the world?
	g. Do you promise to further the peace, unity, and purity of the church?
	h. Will you pray for and seek to serve the people with energy, intelligence, imagination, and love?
	i. (1) (**For ruling elder**) Will you be a faithful ruling elder, watching over the people, providing for their worship, nurture, and service? Will you share in government and discipline, serving in councils of the church, and in your ministry will you try to show the love and justice of Jesus Christ? (2) (**For deacon**) Will you be a faithful deacon, teaching charity, urging concern, and directing the people's help to the friendless and those in need, and in your ministry will you try to show the love and justice of Jesus Christ?

Doctrine and Theology

What Presbyterians Believe (W-4.4003 c)

Do you sincerely receive and adopt the essential tenets of the Reformed faith as expressed in the confessions of our church as authentic and reliable expositions of what Scripture leads us to believe and do, and will you be instructed and led by those confessions as you lead the people of God?

The Bible and Essential Tenets (W-4.4003 b, d)

Will you fulfill your ministry in obedience to Jesus Christ, under the authority of Scripture, and be continually guided by our confessions?

Assignments

Book of Order: F-1, 2
Book of Confessions: prefaces to each confession
Selected to Serve: Chapter 6
Participant Workbook: Study Guide section 2 (2.1–2.15)
Worksheet: To Be or Not to Be—Reformed
Worksheet: *Book of Confessions*
Worksheet: To Be a Christian

Opening Worship

CALL TO WORSHIP

> Leader: The Lord be with you.
>
> **People: And also with you.**

PRAYER OF CONFESSION

> Leader: Lord, I have sinned against you,
>> . . . in thought *(silence)*
>> . . . in word *(silence)*
>> . . . in deed *(silence)*.
>
> **All: Hear my prayer and forgive my sin. Renew within me a right spirit, O God. Through Christ we pray. Amen.**

ASSURANCE OF PARDON

> Leader: In the name of Christ, we are forgiven.
>
> **People: Thanks be to God! Amen.**

SCRIPTURE: Numbers 11:10–17

[10]Moses heard the people weeping throughout their families, all at the entrances of their tents. Then the LORD became very angry, and Moses was displeased. [11]So Moses said to the LORD, "Why have you treated your servant so badly? Why have I not found favor in your sight, that you lay the burden of all this people on me? [12]Did I conceive all this people? Did I give birth to them, that you should say to me, 'Carry them in your bosom, as a nurse carries a sucking child,' to the land that you promised on oath to their ancestors'? [13]Where am I to get meat to give all this people? For they come weeping to me and say, 'Give us meat to eat!' [14]I am not able to carry all this people alone, for they are too heavy for me. [15]If this is the way you are going to treat me, put me to death at once—if I have found favor in your sight—and do not let me see my misery."

[16]So the LORD said to Moses, "Gather for me seventy of the elders of Israel, whom you know to be the elders of the people and leaders over them; bring them to the tent of meeting, and have them take their place there with you. [17]I will come down and talk with you there; and I will take some of the spirit that is on you and put it on them; and they shall bear the burden of the people along with you so that you will not bear it all by yourself.

REFLECTIONS

BIDDING PRAYERS

Response: Lord, hear our prayer.

COMMUNION

THE PEACE

Worksheet: To Be or Not to Be—Reformed!

Instructions

In the column marked "I," evaluate each of the following statements or viewpoints using the following scale:

1 = Definitely a Presbyterian/Reformed point of view
2 = Don't know / can't tell / could be . . .
3 = Definitely NOT a Presbyterian/Reformed point of view

You will be given instructions for additional steps and the use of the other columns in class.

I	G	R	Statement or Viewpoint
			1. Human beings are certainly sinful but God has given humans the freedom to choose between good and evil.
			2. Infants should be baptized as soon as possible so that, if they were to die, they would still be saved and go to heaven.
			3. When you stop your busyness and really focus on listening, then God will speak to you.
			4. Christians should stay out of politics and social issues and focus on developing their own personal relationship to Jesus Christ.
			5. God spoke to humans through the divine words written down as Scripture and has preserved them to reveal God's truth for every age.
			6. The first priority of Christians is to share the good news with others and lead them to Christ.
			7. If we, after helping ourselves as much as we can, reach out to God, God is ready and waiting to help and will reach out to us.
			8. I don't have to go to church to be spiritual, and being a spiritual person is more important that being religious.
			9. Why should I bother going to church if the church isn't meeting my spiritual needs?
			10. The problem with many Christians today is they spend too much energy on trying to make sense of their faith instead of just experiencing God and living their faith.
			11. God looks at the motivations in our hearts. If we try our best and do more good than bad in this life, God will honor our intentions and reward us in heaven.
			12. If people would only read the Bible, they would find answers to all their questions from modern life.

—This worksheet is adapted from an activity in *The Roots of Who We Are*, by Roger Nishioka, Bridge Resources, Louisville, KY, 1997.

Worksheet: *Book of Confessions*

Confession	Date(s)	Location	Historical Context / Issues / Themes
Nicene Creed			
Apostles' Creed			
Scots Confession			
Heidelberg Confession			
Second Helvetic Confession			
Westminster Confession			
Shorter Catechism			
Larger Catechism			
Theological Declaration of Barmen			
Confession of 1967			
Brief Statement of Faith			

Worksheet: To Be a Christian

Instructions

Write out all of your responses. This will help you think through it.

As a group, go around the room and allow each person to choose one of the questions he/she would like to share with the group. As time allows, keep going around the room, selecting more questions from group members.

1. Why do you call yourself a Christian?

_____

_____

_____

2. How did you come to be a Christian?

_____

_____

_____

3. Who or what has been the single most important influence in your Christian life?

_____

_____

_____

4. What has been the most important truth about God in shaping your Christian life?

_____

_____

_____

5. What urges to grow do you feel?

_____

_____

_____

6. What anxieties, questions, or resistance do you feel in relationship to growth in your life with God?

_____

_____

_____

—From Robert H. Ramey Jr., and Ben Campbell Johnson, *Living the Christian Life: A Guide to Reformed Spirituality* (Louisville, KY: Westminster/John Knox Press, 1992), 163.

Governance, Worship, and Discipline

The Presbyterian Way (W-4.4003 e, f, g, h)

Will you be governed by our church's polity, and will you abide by its discipline? Will you be a friend among your colleagues in ministry, working with them, subject to the ordering of God's Word and Spirit?

Will you in your own life seek to follow the Lord Jesus Christ, love your neighbors, and work for the reconciliation of the world?

Do you promise to further the peace, unity, and purity of the church?

Will you pray for and seek to serve the people with energy, intelligence, imagination, and love?

When Things Go Wrong (W-4.4003 e)

Will you be governed by our church's polity, and will you abide by its discipline? Will you be a friend among your colleagues in ministry, working with them, subject to the ordering of God's Word and Spirit?

Assignments

> *Book of Order*: F-3; G-1, 2.01–.0105, 3, 6; W-1, 2, 5; D-1, 2
> *Book of Confessions*: Confession of 1967
> *Selected to Serve*: Chapters 3, 4, 5, 8
> *Participant Workbook:* Study Guide Sections 3, 4, 5
> Worksheet: Presbyterian Principles
> Worksheet: Worship True/False Quiz
> Case Study 1: Maintaining the Purity of the Church

Opening Worship

CALL TO WORSHIP

> Leader: The Lord be with you.
>
> **People: And also with you.**

HYMN: "Let Us Break Bread Together" [513 (PH) / 525 (GTG)]

PRAYER OF CONFESSION

> Leader: God has chosen you to be a leader in the Church.
>
> **Elders: Ruling elders are "persons of wisdom and maturity of faith, having demonstrated skills in leadership and being compassionate in spirit" (G-2.0301).**
>
> **Deacons: Deacons should be "persons of spiritual character, honest repute, exemplary lives, brotherly and sisterly love, sincere compassion, and sound judgment" (G-2.0201).**
>
> Leader: Where is your weakness in being this person? In silence, confess your sin to God and ask God to strengthen you for service. *(Silence.)*

ASSURANCE OF PARDON

> Leader: Have you not known? Have you not heard? The Lord is the everlasting God, the Creator of the ends of the earth. He does not faint or grow weary; his understanding is unsearchable. He gives power to the faint and strengthens the powerless (see Isa. 40:28–29).
>
> **People: In the name of Jesus Christ our sins are forgiven!**
>
> **All: Thanks be to God! Amen.**

SCRIPTURE: Mark 6:30–44

> Narrator: The apostles gathered around Jesus, and told him all that they had done and taught. He said to them,
>
> Jesus: Come away to a deserted place all by yourselves and rest a while.
>
> Narrator: For many were coming and going, and they had no leisure even to eat. And they went away in the boat to a deserted place by themselves. Now many saw them going and recognized them, and they hurried there on foot from all the towns and arrived ahead of them. As he went ashore, he saw a great crowd; and he had compassion for them, because they were like sheep without a shepherd; and he began to teach them many things. When it grew late, his disciples came to him and said,

Disciples: This is a deserted place, and the hour is now very late; send them away so that they may go into the surrounding country and villages and buy something for themselves to eat.

Narrator: But he answered them,

Jesus: You give them something to eat.

Narrator: They said to him,

Disciples: Are we to go and buy two hundred denarii worth of bread, and give it to them to eat?

Narrator: And he said to them,

Jesus: How many loaves have you? Go and see.

Narrator: When they had found out, they said,

Disciples: Five, and two fish.

Narrator: Then he ordered them to get all the people to sit down in groups on the green grass. So they sat down in groups of hundreds and of fifties. Taking the five loaves and the two fish, he looked up to heaven, and blessed and broke the loaves, and gave them to his disciples to set before the people; and he divided the two fish among them all. And all ate and were filled; and they took up twelve baskets full of broken pieces of the fish. Those who had eaten the loaves numbered five thousand men.

REFLECTIONS

BIDDING PRAYERS

Response: Lord, hear our prayer.

COMMUNION

THE PEACE

Worksheet: Presbyterian Principles

Create your paraphrase of each principle that shapes the "Presbyterian way."

Historic Principles of Church Order (F-3.0101–0108)

.0101 _____

.0102 _____

.0103 _____

.0104 _____

.0105 _____

.0106 _____

.0107 _____

.0108 _____

Principles of Presbyterian Government (F-3.0201–.0209)

.0201 _____

.0202 _____

.0203 _____

.0204 _____

.0205 _____

.0206 _____

.0207 _____

.0208 _____

.0209 _____

Summary

Now that you've had a look "behind the curtain," how would you summarize the "Presbyterian way"?

_____

_____

_____

Worksheet: Worship True/False Quiz

_____   1. There can be no worship without mission and outreach.*

_____   2. Being in a particular structure, familiar or not, does not guarantee that people will be treated with Christian love or respect.**

_____   3. As church leaders, we are especially responsible to the church in our prayer life.***

_____   4. Presbyterians celebrate four sacraments: the Lord's Supper, Baptism, Weddings, and Funerals.

_____   5. A sacrament is a holy ordinance instituted by Christ.

_____   6. All children are eligible for baptism.

_____   7. A child being baptized in a Presbyterian Church must have parents who are members of a Presbyterian Church.

_____   8. No one can be excluded from the Lord's Table.

_____   9. Children are not allowed to partake of the Lord's Supper until they are confirmed.

_____   10. Artistic expressions (architecture, furnishings, music, drama, etc.) should evoke, edify, and enhance the worshiper's need for comfort and reassurance of grace. (see W-1.3034 (2))

_____   11. Those responsible for worship are to be guided by the reformed tradition, the tradition of the local congregation, and openness to diversity and inclusive language. (see W-1.4001)

_____   12. In a particular church, the clergy are to provide for worship and shall encourage the people to participate fully and regularly in it. (see W-1.4004)

_____   13. The session has authority to choose Scriptures, lessons to be read, to oversee the prayers offered on behalf of the people, and to choose the music to be sung. (see W-1.4005a)

_____   14. The sequence or proportion of the elements of worship are the responsibility of the session with the concurrence of the pastor. (see W-1.4006)

_____   15. The sermon is the heart of worship. (see W-2.1001)

_____   16. In worship, music is not to be for entertainment or artistic display. (see W-2.1004)

_____   17. The teaching elder has responsibility for the selection of the version of text from which the Scripture lessons are read in public worship. (see W-2.2005)

_____   18. The congregation may read Scripture responsively, antiphonally, or in unison as a part of the service. (see W-2.2006)

_____   19. Only a minister can invite another minister to preach in his or her pulpit. (see W.2.2007)

_____   20. It is possible to be re-baptized if someone has a conversion experience. (see W-2.3009)

_____ 21. Baptism is authorized by the clergy and can be celebrated in private or public worship. (see W-2.3011)

_____ 22. The session assumes responsibility for nurturing the baptized person in the Christian life. (see W-2.3013)

_____ 23. It is appropriate to celebrate the Lord's Supper as often as each Lord's Day. (see W-2.4009)

* Johnson, *Selected to Serve*, 55.
** Ibid., 61.
*** Ibid., 63.

Case Study: Maintaining the Purity of the Church

Joan feared this day would come. The church newsletter she held in her hands had become almost too heavy to hold so she laid it on the breakfast table. The church nominating committee had published the list of nominees for church leadership. Under the ruling elder nominees was the name Cameron Southeby. "What am I going to do now?" she thought to herself.

One morning eight months ago, her schedule had been hectic and she hadn't stopped for lunch until after 2:00 p.m. Joan had heard about a little out-of-the-way bistro and decided to try it. She had been seated for only a few minutes when a couple was seated behind her. She saw Cameron Southeby, a well-known member of her church, take a seat, but he was too interested in his companion to notice her. While their conversation was muted, Joan couldn't help but overhear enough to quickly confirm that Cameron was having an affair. The content of the couple's chat left no room for doubt. Much of the talk centered on how to keep his wife from finding out. Joan lost her appetite and never did get to sample the food.

Sara Southeby was an acquaintance of Joan's, but they had never been close. Still, the knowledge that Cameron was cheating on his wife made Joan ill.

For weeks, Joan struggled with this knowledge. She argued with herself over whether to say anything to Sara. Eventually she concluded that she just couldn't. She would just keep things to herself. It didn't help that, since Cameron was one of the regular adult class teachers, Joan saw him every Sunday in church, meeting and greeting people. His rather high profile in the community as a real estate developer made him a popular man, and he was well known in the church for what most people assumed was his substantial financial support of the church. But Joan saw something different from the public persona.

Having served previously as a church leader in ordered ministry, Joan knew her church avoided making waves, especially when it was hard to get leaders. She understood the practical reality of it, but she was still troubled.

She continued to hear gossip from her non-church friends suggesting the affair was still active. Now seeing his name on the list of nominations for church office created a whole new dilemma. She knew she couldn't vote for him, but should she take a more active role and oppose his election? If she did, it would most certainly disrupt the church and make her a lightning rod for criticism. If she didn't, how could she continue to participate with integrity in a church with leaders like Cameron? Did she have an obligation to tell what she knew? Who would she tell? Maybe it was better to do nothing and assume the church knew what it was doing. But apparently the nominating committee did not know about Cameron's adultery.

The phone rang, startling her out of her moody reflection. Unbelievably, it was the church's pastor, calling to check on a task Joan had assumed some time ago. She tried to find her voice and began to speak . . .

For Discussion

1. What are some of the issues at stake here in terms of Presbyterian polity? Presbyterian theology?
2. What references in the *Book of Order* and/or *Book of Confessions* shed light on the issues?
3. Do you think Joan should tell anyone about what she knows?
    a. If so, why? Who should she tell and how?
    b. If not, why not?
4. Do you believe the church should uphold certain standards for church leaders in ordered ministry different from that required for regular church membership?
    a. If so, how should such standards be maintained?
5. How would you respond to this situation?

The Work of Ministry

What Elders/Deacons Do (W-4.4003 i)

(1) (For ruling elder) Will you be a faithful ruling elder, watching over the people, providing for their worship, nurture, and service? Will you share in government and discipline, serving in councils of the church, and in your ministry will you try to show the love and justice of Jesus Christ?

(2) (For deacon) Will you be a faithful deacon, teaching charity, urging concern, and directing the people's help to the friendless and those in need, and in your ministry will you try to show the love and justice of Jesus Christ?

(3) (For teaching elder) Will you be a faithful teaching elder, proclaiming the good news in Word and Sacrament, teaching faith and caring for people? Will you be active in government and discipline, serving in the councils of the church; and in your ministry will you try to show the love and justice of Jesus Christ?

(4) (For ruling elder commissioned to particular pastoral service) Will you be a faithful ruling elder in this commission, serving the people by proclaiming the good news, teaching faith and caring for the people, and in your ministry will you try to show the love and justice of Jesus Christ?

How This Church Works

Assignments

> *Book of Order:* G-2.01-2.04
> *Book of Confessions:* A Brief Statement of Faith
> *Selected to Serve:* Chapter 9
> *Participant Workbook:* Study Guide section 6 (6.1–6.9); review questions 3.5, 3.6
> Worksheet: Duties of Ordered Ministries
> Worksheet: Writing a Personal Statement of Faith
> Worksheet (optional): Writing Your Financial Stewardship Journey

Opening Worship

CALL TO WORSHIP

>   Leader: The Lord be with you.
>
>   **People: And also with you.**

HYMN (seated): "Come, Holy Spirit, Heavenly Dove" [126 (PH) / 279 (GTG)]

LITANY OF PENITENCE

>   Leader: Let us pray.
>
>   **All: Holy and merciful God,**
>   **we confess to you and to one another,**
>   **and to the whole communion of saints in heaven and on earth,**
>   **that we have sinned by our own fault**
>   **in thought, word, and deed,**
>   **by what we have done,**
>   **and by what we have left undone.**
>
>   Leader: We have not loved you with our whole heart, and mind, and strength.
>   We have not loved our neighbors as ourselves.
>   We have not forgiven others as we have been forgiven.
>
>   **People: Have mercy on us, O God.**
>
>   Leader: We have not listened to your call to serve as Christ served us.
>   We have not been true to the mind of Christ.
>   We have grieved your Holy Spirit.
>
>   **People: Have mercy on us, O God.**
>
>   Leader: We confess to you, O God, all our past unfaithfulness:
>   the pride, hypocrisy, and impatience in our lives,
>
>   **People: we confess to you, O God.**
>
>   Leader: Our self-indulgent appetites and ways and our exploitation of other people,
>
>   **People: we confess to you, O God.**
>
>   Leader: Our anger at our own frustration and our envy
>   of those more fortunate than ourselves,
>
>   **People: we confess to you, O God.**
>
>   Leader: Our intemperate love of worldly goods and comforts,
>   and our dishonesty in daily life and work,
>
>   **People: we confess to you, O God.**
>
>   Leader: Our negligence in prayer and worship,
>   and our failure to commend the faith that is in us,
>
>   **People: we confess to you, O God.**

Leader: Accept our repentance, O God,
for the wrongs we have done.
for our neglect of human need and suffering
and our indifference to injustice and cruelty,

People: accept our repentance, O God.

Leader: For all false judgments,
for uncharitable thoughts toward our neighbors,
and for our prejudice and contempt
toward those who differ from us,

People: accept our repentance, O God.

Leader: For our waste and pollution of your creation
and our lack of concern for those who come after us,

People: accept our repentance, O God.

Leader: Restore us, O God,
and let your anger depart from us.

**All: Favorably hear us, O God,
for your mercy is great. Amen**

ASSURANCE OF PARDON

Leader: Hear the Good News!

People: In Jesus Christ our sins are forgiven!

SCRIPTURE (unison): Ephesians 4:11–16

[11]The gifts he gave were that some would be apostles, some prophets, some evangelists, some pastors and teachers, [12]to equip the saints for the work of ministry, for building up the body of Christ, [13]until all of us come to the unity of the faith and of the knowledge of the Son of God, to maturity, to the measure of the full stature of Christ. [14]We must no longer be children, tossed to and fro and blown about by every wind of doctrine, by people's trickery, by their craftiness in deceitful scheming. [15]But speaking the truth in love, we must grow up in every way into him who is the head, into Christ, [16]from whom the whole body, joined and knit together by every ligament with which it is equipped, as each part is working properly, promotes the body's growth in building itself up in love.

REFLECTIONS

BIDDING PRAYERS

Response: Lord, hear our prayer.

COMMUNION

THE PEACE

—The Litany of Penitence is from *Book of Common Worship* (Louisville, KY: Westminster/John Knox Press, 1993), 225–26.

Worksheet: Duties of Ordered Ministries

For each duty listed, note which ordered ministry has that responsibility. Include references.

Duty	Teaching Elder	Ruling Elder	Deacon
1. Be responsible for the life of a congregation as well as the whole church, including ecumenical relationships			
2. Equip the saints for the work of ministry (Eph. 4:12)			
3. Exercise compassion, witness, and service			
4. Exercise leadership, government, spiritual discernment, and discipline			
5. Help those burdened by unjust policies or structures			
6. Preach the faith of the church			
7. Serve as faithful members of the session			
8. Serve as pastors to support the people in the disciplines of the faith amid the struggles of daily life			
9. Serve as preachers of the Word			
10. Share in the redeeming love of Jesus Christ for the poor, the hungry, the sick, the lost, the friendless, the oppressed, or anyone in distress			
11. Serve as presbyters participating in the responsibilities of governance, seeking always to discern the mind of Christ and to build up Christ's body through devotion, debate, and decision			
12. Administer font and table to interpret the mysteries of grace and lift the people's vision toward the hope of God's new creation			
13. Distribute the bread and wine at Communion			
14. Stand for election as commissioners to higher councils			
15. Provide for nurturing the faith among members			

Worksheet: Writing a Personal Statement of Faith

Each leader-elect, as part of his or her preparation for the examination, will develop a statement of faith to be read and shared as the first part of the examination. The faith statement is one concrete way for current elders to know something of the personal faith of each leader elect.

We ask each person being examined to **bring two copies** of the faith statement with him or her to the examination—**one to turn in** and **one to keep** on file. The faith statements are kept on file with the pastor(s) and are not otherwise distributed.

As one way of helping you understand what a faith statement is, several diverse examples are available at the end of this *Participant's Workbook*.

- A faith statement is not a telling of your faith journey ("I grew up in a Christian home"). It is more like a "confession," articulating what you believe as a person of faith.
- A faith statement is often presented in the form of "I believe . . ."
- A faith statement can be expressed in different forms (narrative and poetry are common).
- A faith statement will often include specific statements of belief in (but not limited to) the following areas:
  - God
  - Jesus Christ
  - The Holy Spirit
  - The Bible
  - The Church
  - One's sense of call, purpose, or mission in the world

Remember to sign and bring two printed (not handwritten) copies of your Faith Statement to the Exam (one to keep in your files and one to turn in to the session).

Worksheet (optional): Writing Your Financial Stewardship Journey

Stewardship of our financial resources is an important part of our spiritual journeys and of the leadership we bring to our congregations. All that we have is God's, and our calling as disciples is to manage our resources in a way that serves Christ, the Church, and God's kingdom mission.

As you prepare for service as a church leader, we ask you to spend some time thinking and praying about your journey of financial stewardship and generosity. This reflection will help you take inventory of your journey—how you have matured as a steward and your continued opportunities for growth—and prepare you to give witness to the truth that living as a faithful steward deepens our relationship with Christ and enables ministry in Christ's name.

Also, to the extent we share our stories, we challenge and help one another grow. In that sharing, we encourage and stimulate discussion of what it means to be generous stewards of our financial resources.

Instructions

Use these questions or tell your story in your own way. Write out a description of your current financial stewardship, how you got here, and where you will go from here.

- Growing up, what was your family's attitude toward giving money to the Church?
- What did they teach you?
- Do you consider your giving as part of your faith journey? If yes, in what way?
- If your thinking has changed, share how it has changed and some of the influences for change.
- Have any specific Scripture verses shaped your thinking? If so, which ones?
- As you think about giving to the Church, do you use a percentage of your income or a flat amount when determining the amount of your pledge?
- How has the process of determining how much you give changed over the years?
- How would you describe where you are on your journey toward generosity?
- Are you content with the amount/percentage you are giving? Why or why not?
- Do you make a distinction between giving to the Church, to Christian non-profits, and to other non-profits? If so, how would you describe the difference?
- Do you have a priority order in giving? If so, why? What distinction do you make among choices?
- Dividing your charitable giving into three categories, with the total equaling 100%, approximately what percent of your total giving goes to each category?

Church	____%
Christian non-profits (e.g., Habitat, Salvation Army, World Vision, Samaritan's Purse, etc.)	____%
All other non-profits (e.g., symphony, university, Red Cross, etc.)	____%
Total should equal	100%

- In what ways, if any, have you made sacrificial gifts or modified or capped your lifestyle in order to increase your giving?
- Have you noticed any differences in your lifestyle or your spiritual life as a result?

Session Exam Guidelines

What to Expect during the Session Exam

You will be examined by the session as a whole or in groups of two or three incoming Ruling Elders and Deacons.

- This will be an oral exam lasting about forty-five minutes.
- First, you will be asked to read aloud your personal Statement of Faith.
  - Bring two copies—one to leave with the Table Moderator.
- Then, you will be examined in the areas required by our Constitution
  - See Constitutional Questions in workshop 1.
- You will be able to bring your Study Guide with you.
- The elders will pose questions primarily from the Study Guide, although they are not limited to the Study Guide for questions
- You are expected to be able to answer the questions posed.
- While you may refer to your Study Guide and notes, you are expected to know the content and should not simply read your answers.

After the exam is completed, the session will take a break during which the elders will confer on the examination, making note of any incoming leaders not prepared to be installed into his or her ordered ministry.

- If an incoming leader is judged to be unprepared, remedial work will be required before ordination/installation.

The session will reconvene and take action to certify the incoming leaders who are ready for ordination/installation. Then they will handle any remaining business. A brief worship service including Communion will be a part of the session meeting. Incoming leaders are expected to stay for the remainder of the meeting.

Leader Development Post-Class Evaluation

Name: _____ Date: _____

We ask for your name so we can track who has completed the survey. Your responses to this survey will be compiled anonymously.

Topic	Rating
1. Now, at the end of your training, to what extent do you feel prepared to assume your ministry? **1**=not prepared <==> **5**=very prepared	
Comments: _____ _____	
2. We are all at different places on the journey of faith and readiness to serve as leaders in ministry. For each specific area listed, rate your sense of preparedness, now that you have completed this training process. **1**=not prepared <==> **5**=very prepared	
My personal faith	
My knowledge of PC(USA) doctrine	
My knowledge of PC(USA) governance	
My knowledge of PC(USA) discipline	
My understanding of the duties of ruling elders and deacons	
My readiness as a spiritual leader	
Comments: _____ _____ _____	
3. At the end of this training course, how would you assess your current enthusiasm for serving as a ruling elder or deacon? **1**=very apprehensive <==> **5**=very enthusiastic	
Comments: _____ _____ _____	

4. Rate the following elements of your leader training. **1**=Not Helpful <=> **5**=Extremely Helpful	
Worship / Communion	
Assigned readings	
Small group work / activities	
Individual worksheets	
Study Guide	
Session exam by elders	
5. To what extent were you able to complete these course assignments? **1**=few <=> **5**=nearly all	
Study Guide questions	
Selected to Serve readings	
Book of Order readings	
Book of Confessions readings	
Worksheets prepared individually before class	
Supplemental readings	

6. What feedback do you have on the amount of or depth of homework assigned and its helpfulness in this training?

_____

_____

_____

_____

7. My most significant learning(s) / experience(s) in this course was/were . . .

_____

_____

_____

8. Some of the least helpful/significant aspects of this course were (and your suggestions for improvement) . . .

_____

_____

_____

_____

9. How would you rate the facilitators / leaders of this course?

    1=very poor <=> **5**=excellent

Comments:

_____

_____

_____

10. For your continuing education as a leader, in which of the following would you be willing to participate? (check all that apply)

Occasional Sunday School classes for leaders	
Short-term mid-week classes	
Weekly reading articles	
Monthly reading articles	

Comments and/or Suggestions:

_____

_____

_____

_____

11. Is there anything else you would like those planning for next year's class to know?

_____

_____

_____

_____

_____

Supplemental Resources

Constitutional Questions for Ordination and Installation: Content Areas

Question	Content Area
W-4.4003a. Do you trust in Jesus Christ your Savior, acknowledge him Lord of all and Head of the Church, and through him believe in one God, Father, Son, and Holy Spirit?	**Personal Faith**
W-4.4003b. Do you accept the Scriptures of the Old and New Testaments to be, by the Holy Spirit, the unique and authoritative witness to Jesus Christ in the Church universal, and God's Word to you? (2 Tim. 3:16; Eph. 2:20)	**Doctrine** The Authority of Scripture
W-4.4003c. Do you sincerely receive and adopt the essential tenets of the Reformed faith as expressed in the confessions of our church as authentic and reliable expositions of what Scripture leads us to believe and do, and will you be instructed and led by those confessions as you lead the people of God? (2 Tim. 1:13) **W-4.4003d.** Will you fulfill your ministry in obedience to Jesus Christ, under the authority of Scripture, and be continually guided by our confessions?	**Doctrine** Theology, the Confessions, and Authority in the Church
W-4.4003e. Will you be governed by our church's polity, and will you abide by its discipline? Will you be a friend among your colleagues in ministry, working with them, subject to the ordering of God's Word and Spirit? (1 Pet. 5:5)	**Governance and Discipline** **Collegial Ministry**
W-4.4003f. Will you in your own life seek to follow the Lord Jesus Christ, love your neighbors, and work for the reconciliation of the world? **W-4.4003g.** Do you promise to further the peace, unity, and purity of the church? **W-4.4003h.** Will you pray for and seek to serve the people with energy, intelligence, imagination, and love?	**Personal Faith / Individual Commitment**
W-4.4003i (1). (For ruling elder) Will you be a faithful ruling elder, watching over the people, providing for their worship, nurture, and service? Will you share in government and discipline, serving in councils of the church, and in your ministry will you try to show the love and justice of Jesus Christ? **W-4.4003i (2).** (For deacon) Will you be a faithful deacon, teaching charity, urging concern, and directing the people's help to the friendless and those in need, and in your ministry will you try to show the love and justice of Jesus Christ?	**Governance and Discipline** **Duties of the Ministry**

Some Essential Tenets of the Reformed Faith

Tradition	Tenet / Belief / Doctrine
Catholic (universal)	1. **Trinity**—the mystery of the triune God as Father, Son, and Holy Spirit
	2. **Incarnation** —of the eternal Word of God in Jesus Christ
Protestant	3. **Justification by grace through faith** —grace alone, faith alone
	4. **Scripture** reveals God's grace in Jesus Christ —Scripture alone
Reformed	5. **Sovereignty of God** —the majesty, holiness, and providence of God who creates, sustains, rules, and redeems the world in the freedom of sovereign righteousness and love
	6. **Election for service and salvation** —love of neighbor as well as love of God
	7. **Covenant life** —marked by disciplined concern for order in the church according to the Word of God
	8. **Stewardship** —that shuns ostentation and seeks proper use of the gifts of God's creation
	9. **Human tendency toward idolatry and tyranny** —which calls the people of God to work for the transformation of society by seeking justice and living in obedience to the Word of God

—From the *Book of Order* F-2.0300–2.0500.

Guidelines for Understanding and Use of Holy Scripture

1. Determining What the Text Says

    a. Use of the Original Languages

    b. Employment of the Best Manuscripts

    c. Priority of the Plain Sense of the Text

        1) Definition of Literary Units

        2) Recognition of the Cultural Conditioning of Language

        3) Understanding of Social and Historical Circumstances

2. How the Text Is Rightly Used

    a. Purpose of Holy Scripture

    b. Precedence of Holy Scripture

        1) Priority of Holy Scripture

        2) Use of Knowledge

        3) Use of Experience

    c. Centrality of Jesus Christ

    d. Interpretation of Scripture by Scripture

    e. The Rule of Love

    f. The Rule of Faith

    g. Fallibility of All Interpretation

    h. Relation of Word and Spirit

    i. Use of All Relevant Guidelines

For Interpreting

1. Be guided by the basic rules for the interpretation of Scripture that are summarized from the *Book of Confessions.*

    a. Recognize that Jesus Christ is the center of Scripture.

    b. Let the focus be on the plain text of Scripture, to the grammatical and historical context, rather than to allegory or subjective fantasy.

    c. Depend upon the guidance of the Holy Spirit in interpreting and applying God's message.

    d. Be guided by the doctrinal consensus of the church, which is the rule of faith.

    e. Let all interpretations be in accord with the rule of love, the twofold commandment to love God and to love neighbor.

    f. Remember that interpretation of the Bible requires earnest study in order to establish the best text and to interpret the influence of the historical and cultural context in which the divine message has come.

    g. Seek to interpret a particular passage of the Bible in light of all of the Bible.

2. Recognize that individual perceptions of the truth are always limited and therefore not absolutely authoritative.

3. Realize that points of view are conditioned by points of viewing—try to see the issues from the perspectives of others. Can differences be preserved in ways that lead toward mutual understanding?

4. The preached word must inform the study of the written word—the search for truth includes the life of public prayer and worship.

5. In the immediate situation when controversy arises, locate areas of agreement and disagreement.

   a. Is there agreement as to what biblical passages are relevant to the contemporary issue?

   b. Is there agreement to the meaning of those texts in their original setting?

   c. Is there agreement as to how these texts should be applied to the present situation?

   d. Is there agreement as to what the Christian tradition in general and the Reformed Tradition in particular have taught concerning this issue?

6. In potentially long-term controversies, covenant together to study the Bible in regard to the issue—ensuring openness to differing opinions.

7. Together try to determine the range of options that are open to the church for speech and action in regard to the contemporary situation.

8. Rely on the democratic process of the denomination in assemblies—use the established channels of communication and the process of voting to express conviction, either as part of the majority or the minority. Be willing to accept decisions and welcome the continuing advocacy of minority views.

—Summaries of *Presbyterian Understanding and Use of Holy Scripture* (a position statement adopted by the 123rd General Assembly(1983) of the Presbyterian Church in the United States) and *Biblical Authority and Interpretation* (a resource document received by the 194th General Assembly (1982) of the United Presbyterian Church in the United States of America).

Comparison of Distinctive Emphases of the Reformed Faith

A number of ways of defining the distinctive emphases or "essence" of the Reformed faith have been proposed both formally and informally through the centuries. The following are a small sample of the proposals.

The Ethos of the Reformed Tradition

- The Majesty and Praise of God
- The Polemic against Idolatry
- The Working Out of the Divine Purposes in History
- Ethics, a Life of Holiness
- The Life of the Mind as the Service of God
- Preaching
- The Organized Church and Pastoral Care
- The Disciplined Life
- Simplicity

—John H. Leith, *An Introduction to the Reformed Tradition: A Way of Being the Christian Community*, rev. ed. (Atlanta: John Knox Press, 1981), chap. 3.

On Being Reformed

- God-Centered
- A People of the Word
- The Correlation of Word and Spirit
- The Covenant, the Clue to Scripture
- Church Order
- Doctrine with a Purpose
- A Life and World View

—From I. John Hesselink, *On Being Reformed: Distinctive Characteristics and Common Misunderstandings* (Ann Arbor, MI: Servant Books, 1983), chap. 13.

The Reformed Imperative

- Mystery and Revelation
- The Power of God unto Salvation
- God's Providing, Ordering, and Caring
- Chosen before the Foundation of the World
- A New Heaven and a New Earth
- The Presence and the Power of God

—From John H. Leith, *The Reformed Imperative: What the Church Has to Say That No One Else Can Say* (Philadelphia: Westminster Press, 1988), chaps. 2–7.

Consider the Distinctive

"Reformed theology lives from stressing the prior initiative of God and our grateful response. This is the Reformed faith's inclination, its bent, its proclivity. This is Reformed theology's tendency and impetus in understanding Scripture and doing Christian theology. It is not a 'central dogma' as such—a single 'Reformed' formulation, which in and of itself provides the ordering structural motif for a Reformed 'system of doctrine.' It is rather a Reformed direction throughout doctrines. Each one, interrelating with others, shares this trajectory in common. The Reformed affirmation is toward seeing in all theological declarations that God is prior, God acts; that humans respond, and respond as grateful persons. Where the Reformed faith has interacted theologically with other traditions and views, it has done so by upholding this contention as the basis for its positive theological statements as well as in its critiques of other positions."

—From Donald K. McKim, "The 'Heart and Center' of the Reformed Faith," *Reformed Review*, 51, no. 3 (Spring 1998):208–9.

The Bible in Our Confessions

The Westminster Confession

1640s, The Holy Scripture

6.001   Although the light of nature, and the works of creation and providence, do so far manifest the goodness, wisdom, and power of God, as to leave men inexcusable; yet are they not sufficient to give that knowledge of God, and of his will, which is necessary unto salvation; therefore it pleased the Lord, at sundry times, and in divers manners, to reveal himself, and to declare that his will unto his Church; and afterwards for the better preserving and propagating of the truth, and for the more sure establishment and comfort of the Church against the corruption of the flesh, and the malice of Satan and of the world, to commit the same wholly unto writing; which maketh the Holy Scripture to be most necessary; those former ways of God's revealing his will unto his people being now ceased.

6.004   The authority of the Holy Scripture, for which it ought to be believed and obeyed, dependeth not upon the testimony of any man or church, but wholly upon God (who is truth itself), the author thereof; and therefore it is to be received, because it is the Word of God.

6.005   We may be moved and induced by the testimony of the Church to an high and reverent esteem for the Holy Scripture; and the heavenliness of the matter, the efficacy of the doctrine, the majesty of the style, the consent of all the parts, the scope of the whole (which is to give all glory to God), the full discovery it makes of the only way of man's salvation, the many other incomparable excellencies, and the entire perfection thereof, are arguments whereby it doth abundantly evidence itself to be the Word of God; yet, notwithstanding, our full persuasion and assurance of the infallible truth and divine authority thereof, is from the inward work of the Holy Spirit, bearing witness by and with the Word in our hearts.

6.009   The infallible rule of interpretation of Scripture, is the Scripture itself; and therefore, when there is a question about the true and full sense of any scripture (which is not manifold, but one), it may be searched and known by other places that speak more clearly.

6.010   The Supreme Judge, by which all controversies of religion are to be determined, and all decrees of councils, opinions of ancient writers, doctrines of men, and private spirits, are to be examined, and in whose sentence we are to rest, can be no other but the Holy Spirit speaking in the Scripture.

The Confession of 1967

Section C, 2. The Bible

9.27   The one sufficient revelation of God is Jesus Christ, the Word of God incarnate, to whom the Holy Spirit bears unique and authoritative witness through the Holy Scriptures, which are received and obeyed as the word of God written. The Scriptures are not a witness among others, but the witness without parallel. The church has received the books of the Old and New Testaments as prophetic and apostolic testimony in which it hears the word of God and by which its faith and obedience are nourished and regulated.

9.28   The New Testament is the recorded testimony of apostles to the coming of the Messiah, Jesus of Nazareth, and the sending of the Holy Spirit to the Church. The Old Testament bears witness to God's faithfulness in his covenant with Israel and points the way to the fulfillment of his purpose in Christ. The Old Testament is indispensable to understanding the New, and is not itself fully understood without the New.

9.29   The Bible is to be interpreted in the light of its witness to God's work of reconciliation in Christ. The Scriptures, given under the guidance of the Holy Spirit, are nevertheless the words of men, conditioned by the language, thought forms, and literary fashions of the places and times at which they were written. They reflect views of life, history, and the cosmos which were then current. The church, therefore, has an obligation to approach the Scriptures with literary and historical understanding. As God has spoken his word in diverse cultural situations, the church is confident that he will continue to speak through the Scriptures in a changing world and in every form of human culture.

9.30   God's word is spoken to his church today where the Scriptures are faithfully preached and attentively read in dependence on the illumination of the Holy Spirit and with readiness to receive their truth and direction.

The Declaration of Faith

Chapter Six—The Word of God, PC(USA) (1985)[*]

(3) The Bible is the written Word of God.
Led by the Spirit of God
    the people of Israel and of the early church
    preserved and handed on the story
    of what God had said and done in their midst
    and how they had responded to him.
These traditions were often shaped and reshaped
    by the uses to which the community put them.
They were cherished, written down, and collected
    as the holy literature of the people of God.
Through the inward witness of the same Spirit
    we acknowledge the authority of the Bible.
We accept the Old and New Testaments as the canon,
    or authoritative standard of faith and life,
    to which no further writings need be added.
The Scriptures of the Old and New Testaments
    are necessary, sufficient, and reliable
    as witnesses to Jesus Christ, the living Word.
We must test any word that comes to us
    from church, world, or inner experience
    by the Word of God in Scripture.
We are subject to its judgment
    all our understanding of doctrine and practice,
    including this Declaration of Faith.
We believe the Bible to be the Word of God
    as no other word written by human beings.
Relying on the Holy Spirit,

who opens our eyes and hearts,
    we affirm our freedom to interpret Scripture responsibly.
God has chosen to address his inspired Word to us
    through diverse and varied human writings.
Therefore we use the best available methods
    to understand them in their historical
    and cultural settings
    and the literary forms in which they are cast.
When we encounter apparent tensions and conflicts
    in what Scripture teaches us to believe and do,
    the final appeal must be to the authority of Christ.
Acknowledging that authority,
    comparing Scripture with Scripture,
    listening with respect to fellow-believers past and present,
we anticipate that the Holy Spirit
    will enable us to interpret faithfully
God's Word for our time and place.

*The 197th General Assembly (PCUSA, 1985) made its own the action of the 177th General Assembly (PCUS, 1977) with reference to A Declaration of Faith, which is as follows: "That 'A Declaration of Faith' be adopted as a contemporary statement of faith, a reliable aid for Christian study, liturgy, and inspiration . . ." (Minutes, PCUS, 1977, Part I, p. 168), with the understanding that only the current *Book of Confessions* has constitutional standing.

The Study Catechism: Confirmation Version

Approved by the 210th General Assembly (1998)

Question 45. *What do you mean when you speak of "the Word of God"?*

"Jesus Christ as he is attested for us in Holy Scripture is the one Word of God whom we have to hear, and whom we have to trust and obey in life and in death" (Barmen Declaration, Article I).

Question 46. *Isn't Holy Scripture also the Word of God?*

Yes. Holy Scripture is also God's Word because of its focus, its function and its founder. Its central focus is Jesus Christ, the living Word. Its basic function is to deepen our love, knowledge and service of him as our Savior and Lord. And its dependable founder is the Holy Spirit, who spoke through the prophets and apostles, and who inspires us with eager desire for the truths that Scripture contains.

Question 47. *Isn't preaching also the Word of God?*

Yes. Preaching is God's Word when it is faithful to the witness of Holy Scripture. Faith comes by hearing God's Word in the form of faithful preaching and teaching.

Life Together in the Community of Faith: Standards of Ethical Conduct for Ordained Leaders in the Presbyterian Church (U.S.A.)

As an ordained leader in the Presbyterian Church (U.S.A.), in obedience to Jesus Christ, under the authority of Scripture and guided by our Confessions, I affirm the vows made at my ordination, confirm that Jesus Christ is the pattern for my life and ministry and, relying on God's grace, commit myself to the following standards of ethical conduct.

I

I will conduct my life in a manner that is faithful to the gospel and consistent with my public ministry. Therefore I will:

1. Practice the disciplines of study, prayer, reflection, worship, stewardship, and service;
2. Be honest and truthful in my relationships with others;
3. Be faithful, keeping the covenants I make and honoring marriage vows;
4. Treat all persons with equal respect and concern as beloved children of God;
5. Maintain a healthy balance among the responsibilities of my ministry, my commitments to family and other primary relationships, and my need for spiritual, physical, emotional, and intellectual renewal;
6. Refrain from abusive, addictive, or exploitative behavior and seek help to overcome such behavior if it occurs;
7. Refrain from gossip and abusive speech; and
8. Maintain an attitude of repentance, humility, and forgiveness, responsive to God's reconciling will.

II

I will conduct my ministry so that nothing need be hidden from a governing body or colleagues in ministry. Therefore I will:

1. Preach, teach, and bear witness to the gospel of Jesus Christ with courage, speaking the truth in love;
2. Honor the sacred trust of relationships within the covenant community and observe appropriate boundaries;
3. Be judicious in the exercise of the power and privileges of my ministry and positions of responsibility I hold;
4. Avoid conflicts of interest that might compromise the effectiveness of my ministry;
5. Refrain from exploiting relationships within the community of faith for personal gain or gratification, including sexual harassment and misconduct as defined by Presbyterian Church (U.S.A.) policy;
6. Respect the privacy of individuals and not divulge information obtained in confidence without express permission, unless an individual is a danger to self or others;
7. Recognize the limits of my own gifts and training, and refer persons and tasks to others as appropriate;
8. Claim only those qualifications actually attained, give appropriate credit for all sources used in sermons, papers, music, and presentations, and observe copyrights;
9. Refrain from incurring indebtedness that might compromise my ministry;
10. Be a faithful steward of and fully account for funds and property entrusted to me;
11. Observe limits set by the appropriate governing body for honoraria, personal business endeavors, and gifts or loans from persons other than family;

12. Accept the discipline of the church and the appropriate guidance of those to whom I am accountable for my ministry;
13. Participate in continuing education and seek the counsel of mentors and professional advisors;
14. Deal honorably with the record of my predecessor and upon leaving a ministry speak and act in ways that support the ministry of my successor;
15. **Participate in the life of a ministry setting I left or from which I have retired only as directed by presbytery;
16. **Provide pastoral services for a congregation I previously served only as directed by the presbytery and provide pastoral services to members of other congregations only with the consent of their pastors; and
17. **Consult with the committee on ministry in the presbytery of my residence regarding my involvement in any ministry setting during my retirement.

III

I will participate as a partner with others in the ministry and mission of the Church universal. Therefore I will:

1. Participate in the mission and governance of the Presbyterian Church (U.S.A.) and work for the unity of the holy catholic church;
2. Show respect and provide encouragement for colleagues in ministry;
3. Recruit church members responsibly, respect existing congregational relationships, and refrain from exploiting persons in vulnerable situations; and
4. Cooperate with those working in the world for justice, compassion, and peace, including partners in ministry of other faith traditions.

** These standards apply only to pastors; they also apply to commissioned lay pastors when they are performing pastoral functions.
—Excerpted from the report: "Life Together in the Community of Faith: Standards of Ethical Conduct for Members of the Presbyterian Church (U.S.A.); Standards of Ethical Conduct for Employees and Volunteers of the Presbyterian Church (U.S.A.); and Standards of Ethical Conduct for Ordained Officers in the Presbyterian Church (U.S.A.)," 210th General Assembly, 1998.

Seeking to Be Faithful Together: Guidelines for Presbyterians during Times of Disagreement

Adopted by the 204th General Assembly (1992)

In a spirit of trust and love, we promise we will . . .

Give Them a Hearing Before We Answer [John 7:51 and Proverbs 18:13]

1. Treat other respectfully so as to build trust, believing that we all desire to be faithful to Jesus the Christ;
   - we will keep our conversations and communications open for candid and forthright exchange.
   - we will not ask questions or make statements in a way that will intimidate or judge others.
2. Learn about various positions on the topic of disagreement.
3. State what we think we heard and ask for clarification before responding, in an effort to be sure we understand each other.

Speak the Truth in Love [Ephesians 4:15]

4. Share our concerns directly with individuals or groups with whom we have disagreements in a spirit of love and respect in keeping with Jesus' teaching.
5. Focus on ideas and suggestions instead of questioning people's motives, intelligence or integrity; we will not engage in name-calling or labeling of others prior to, during, or following the discussion.
6. Share our personal experiences about the subject of disagreement so that others may more fully understand our concerns.

Maintain the Unity of the Spirit in the Bond of Peace [Ephesians 4:3]

7. Indicate where we agree with those of other viewpoints as well as where we disagree. Seek to stay in community with each other though the discussion may be vigorous and full of tension;
   - we will be ready to forgive and be forgiven.
8. Follow these additional Guidelines when we meet in decision-making bodies:
   - urge persons of various points of view to speak and promise to listen to these positions seriously;
   - seek conclusions informed by our points of agreement;
   - be sensitive to the feelings and concerns of those who do not agree with the majority and respect their rights of conscience;
   - abide by the decision of the majority, and,
   - if we disagree with it and wish to change it, work for that change in ways which are consistent with these *Guidelines*.
9. Include our disagreements in our prayers, not praying for the triumph of our viewpoints, but seeking God's grace to listen attentively, to speak clearly, and remain open to the vision God holds for us all.

The Prayer of Examen

The Prayer of Examen is an ancient discipline of prayer that heightens a sense of God's presence in our lives. If you have ever hoped to know God's leading as you wrestle with difficult questions or circumstances, this practice can open your heart and mind to God.

The Examen Process	Suggestions
1. Seek to be more aware of God's love surrounding you.	• Adopt a prayerful posture. • Breathe deeply and slowly as if inhaling God's steadfast love. • As best you can, quiet your body and your mind.
2. In silence, take about five minutes to reflect on two questions: a. What has happened today for which I am **most grateful**? b. What has happened today for which I am **least grateful**?	Alternatively: • Where and how did I experience love today? • Where and how did I get energy? • Get drained of energy? • With whom was I most connected? • Most estranged? • Where did I find joy? • Experience sadness? • What were today's highs and low? • When and where were my efforts aligned with • God's purpose? • When and where did they diverge? • For what or to whom do I need to express gratitude?
3. Remember those things for which you are grateful and offer a silent prayer of thanks.	

4. To the extent you are willing, share your reflections with others in your group.	• How was God speaking to you in this time?
	• What insights has God revealed?
	• What things, if any, would you like others to remember in their prayers?
	   − To celebrate with you . . .
	   − To support you . . .

5. After everyone has had an opportunity to share, pray the Lord's Prayer.	

—This exercise is adapted from http://www.thefellowship.info/Pray/Prayer-Practices/Examen, a resource of the Cooperative Baptist Fellowship.

Alternate Worksheets

Authority in the Church

Listed below are five authorities significant for influencing and determining the life and witness of the Church. For each column, number the five authorities in rank order
(**1=most** authoritative to **5=least** authoritative) according to the following:

Column A Based on your experience in this and other churches, to what extent is each authority **actually used** in making decisions?

Column S Based on your personal understanding of church life, to what extent **should** each authority **be used** in directing the life and witness of the church?

Column P Based on your understanding of the Reformed/Presbyterian tradition, how important is each authority **for Presbyterians**?

A	S	P	Authority
			The **Bible**—the Written Word of God as Revealed through the Holy Spirit
			Jesus Christ—the Living Word of God
			The **Essential Tenets of the Reformed Faith** as found in the *Book of Confessions* and the *Book of Order*
			An individual's **Private Understanding and Personal Experience** as he or she faithfully seeks God's will
			The **Testimony and Experience of the Church**, especially as declared in confessions of faith and in official guidance of Church councils/governing bodies

Becoming a Church Leader

What are some of the reasons that you decided to accept a nomination as a church leader at this particular time in your life?

_____

_____

_____

_____

What are some of the life experiences (in the church and outside the church) that have prepared you for service as a leader?

_____

_____

_____

_____

What are some of your hopes for what the church can become or do in your time as a leader?

_____

_____

_____

_____

Everything You Ever Wanted to Know about Ruling Elders and Deacons

True or False

_____ 1. Deacons and elders serve under the mandate of the session.

_____ 2. The ordered ministries (deacon/elder) are gifts to the church to minister and care for the congregation in whatever needs it may have.

_____ 3. The call to ordered ministry in the Church is the act of the Nominating Committee and congregation.

_____ 4. Those being nominated to serve an ordered ministry in the church should meet six basic qualifications.

_____ 5. Candidates for elder/deacon should be examined on their knowledge of the Bible, the organization of their particular church, and their positions on certain social issues.

_____ 6. To be an ordained leader of the church is to exercise freedom of conscience within certain bounds.

_____ 7. The ministry of the deacons is to be determined by the session. Deacons perform all duties of the church that the elders cannot or choose not to perform.

_____ 8. Ruling elders, together with teaching elders, exercise leadership, government, spiritual discernment, and discipline and have responsibilities for the life of a congregation as well as the whole church, including ecumenical relationships.

_____ 9. A Nominating Committee must consist of six members, three men, three women, one of whom must be an elder serving on the session, one a deacon currently serving, and the pastor.

_____ 10. It is not necessary for all newly elected leaders to participate in a training program, but they must be approved by the session as qualified to hold ministry before the congregation elects them.

_____ 11. The Nominating Committee must choose from persons who have been active members for at least one year.

_____ 12. Neither a husband and wife, nor any two people from the same family, can serve on the session or diaconate at the same time.

Foundations of Presbyterian Polity

From your readings, fill in the blanks and cite the reference:	Reference (e.g., F-1.0200)
The Mission of the Church	
1. In Christ, the Church participates in God's mission for the _____ of _____ and _____ by proclaiming the good news of God's _____, offering to all people the _____ of God at font and table, and calling all people to _____ in Christ. 2. God . . . has made _____ the Head of the Church, which is _____ _____. 3. Christ alone _____, _____, _____, and _____ the Church as he wills. 4. Christ gives to the Church its _____ and life, its _____ and mission, its _____ and discipline.	
The Calling of the Church	
5. The Church [as the body of Christ] is to be a community of _____, . . . _____ . . . _____, . . . and _____.	
The Marks of the Church	
6. With all Christians of the Church catholic, we affirm that the Church is "_____, _____, _____, and _____."	
The Notes of the Reformed Church	
Reformed Christians have marked the presence of the true Church whenever 7. The Word of God is _____ _____ and _____. 8. The Sacraments are _____ _____. 9. Ecclesiastical discipline is _____ _____.	
The Great Ends of the Church	
10. The proclamation of the _____ for the _____ of humankind. 11. The _____, _____, and _____ fellowship of the children of God. 12. The maintenance of divine _____. 13. The preservation of the _____. 14. The promotion of social _____. 15. The exhibition of the _____ of _____ to the world.	

Jesus Christ Is Lord

Read the passage below. The key verse is in **bold** typeface.

Romans 10:5–17 Salvation Is for All

[5]Moses writes concerning the righteousness that comes from the law, that "the person who does these things will live by them." [6]But the righteousness that comes from faith says, "Do not say in your heart, 'Who will ascend into heaven?'" (that is, to bring Christ down) [7]"or 'Who will descend into the abyss?'" (that is, to bring Christ up from the dead). [8]But what does it say?

"The word is near you,
    on your lips and in your heart"

(that is, the word of faith that we proclaim); [9]**because if you confess with your lips that Jesus is Lord and believe in your heart that God raised him from the dead, you will be saved.** [10]For one believes with the heart and so is justified, and one confesses with the mouth and so is saved. [11]The scripture says, "No one who believes in him will be put to shame." [12]For there is no distinction between Jew and Greek; the same Lord is Lord of all and is generous to all who call on him. [13]For, "Everyone who calls on the name of the Lord shall be saved."

[14]But how are they to call on one in whom they have not believed? And how are they to believe in one of whom they have never heard? And how are they to hear without someone to proclaim him? [15]And how are they to proclaim him unless they are sent? As it is written, "How beautiful are the feet of those who bring good news!" [16]But not all have obeyed the good news; for Isaiah says, "Lord, who has believed our message?" [17]So faith comes from what is heard, and what is heard comes through the word of Christ.

Questions for Reflection

1. What do Christians mean when they say that Jesus Christ is my Lord and Savior?

_____

_____

_____

_____

_____

_____

2. In your opinion, is Christianity the only true religion?

_____

_____

_____

_____

_____

3. What is meant by "Everyone who calls upon the name of the Lord shall be saved"?

_____

_____

_____

_____

4. In your opinion, how will God deal with the followers of other religions?

_____

_____

_____

_____

Justification by Faith—Grace Alone, Faith Alone

A. The Experience of Salvation

In Acts 9:1–19, the story of Saul's conversion to become the Apostle Paul is told. It is a dramatic story of blinding lights, voices from heaven, and a life-changing encounter with the risen Christ on the road to Damascus. This story represents one model of salvation experience—the dramatic conversion.

In 2 Timothy 1:5, the same Paul acknowledges the multigenerational nature of Timothy's faith, which was passed on from grandmother to mother to son. Paul's protégé, Timothy, represents another model of salvation experience—Christian nurture from birth.

In small groups, each person in turn will take three minutes to share his or her responses to three of the following questions:

1. Is your personal experience of salvation more like that of Paul's (conversion) or like Timothy's (nurture)?
2. What do you remember (or know) about your baptism?
3. Were you confirmed? If so, to what extent was that experience of joining the church your own doing or the doing of others? If not, how would you describe the faith of your early teens?
4. As an adult, to what extent have you consciously and deliberately "claimed" faith in Jesus Christ as your Lord and Savior?

Read Romans 1:16–17:

[16]For I am not ashamed of the gospel; it is the power of God for salvation to everyone who has faith, to the Jew first and also to the Greek. [17]For in it the righteousness of God is revealed through faith for faith; as it is written, "The one who is righteous will live by faith."

Read Romans 3:21–26:

[21]But now, apart from law, the righteousness of God has been disclosed, and is attested by the law and the prophets, [22]the righteousness of God through faith in Jesus Christ for all who believe. For there is no distinction, [23]since all have sinned and fall short of the glory of God; [24]they are now justified by his grace as a gift, through the redemption that is in Christ Jesus, [25]whom God put forward as a sacrifice of atonement by his blood, effective through faith. He did this to show his righteousness, because in his divine forbearance he had passed over the sins previously committed; [26]it was to prove at the present time that he himself is righteous and that he justifies the one who has faith in Jesus.

In small groups, each person in turn will take three minutes to share his or her responses to the following questions:

1. In the relationship between God and human beings, what is the problem? What are we being saved from?
2. What is the solution to this problem? What saves us?
3. What is required of human beings to be saved?

B. Grace Alone, Faith Alone

- The Protestant break from Roman Catholicism—see F-2.04, The Confessions as Statements of the Faith of the Protestant Reformation
- Martin Luther (in his *Preface to Romans*):

[T]he knowledge that we are saved by the love of God in Jesus Christ gives the church extraordinary courage in the most difficult circumstances. Faith is not something dreamed of, a human illusion, but is that which God effects in us. Faith is an unshakable confidence, a belief in the grace of God so assured that a person could die a thousand deaths for its sake. It makes us joyful, high spirited, and eager in our relations with God and all other people.

- Second Helvetic Confession—see C-5.110
- Westminster Standards—see C-6.019; 6.043; 6.068–6.074; C-7.033; C-7.180–83
- Theological Declaration of Barmen—see C-8.15
- Confession of 1967—see C-9.09
- A Brief Statement of Faith—see 10.4 (line 54ff)

How can Presbyterians answer when asked, "When were you saved?"

- "Two thousand years ago—when Jesus died on the cross and was raised from the dead!"
- For Presbyterians, salvation is always about what God has done and is doing, not about what we as humans have done and are doing.

> There is nothing that we can say, do, think, or believe,
>   that will ever make God love us more.
> There is nothing that we can say, do, think, or believe,
>   that will ever make God love us less.
> Such is the amazing grace God has demonstrated in Jesus Christ.

- Grace is the gift of God that creates our faith.

  What we do and how we live in response to that grace is our gift to God.

Marks of Ministry in Congregations

(G-1.0304)

Membership in the Church of Jesus Christ is a joy and a privilege. It is also a commitment to participate in Christ's mission. A faithful member bears witness to God's love and grace and promises to be involved responsibly in the ministry of Christ's Church.

Note your opinion for each of these item using the following scale:
1=highest priority, **2**=high priority, **3**=medium priority, **4**=low priority, **5**=lowest priority

In column **A**, what priority does this item have in **your** regular participation in this church?
In column **B**, what priority does this item have in **your congregation's** day-to-day ministry?
In column **C**, what priority should this item have in the ministry of the **PC(USA)** in the world?

A	B	C	Such involvement includes:
			proclaiming the good news in word and deed,
			taking part in the common life and worship of a congregation,
			lifting one another up in prayer, mutual concern, and active support,
			studying Scripture and the issues of Christian faith and life,
			supporting the ministry of the church through the giving of money, time, and talents,
			demonstrating a new quality of life within and through the church,
			responding to God's activity in the world through service to others,
			living responsibly in the personal, family, vocational, political, cultural, and social relationships of life,
			working in the world for peace, justice, freedom, and human fulfillment,
			participating in the governing responsibilities of the church, and
			reviewing and evaluating regularly the integrity of one's membership, and considering ways in which one's participation in the worship and service of the church may be increased and made more meaningful.

Leader Experience Assessment

Mark all that apply

1. Our session spends much of its time
    a. Making rules, setting policy
    b. Managing its committee's work
    c. Nurturing the spiritual development of elders
2. Our session tends to
    a. Ignore the small stuff
    b. Micro-manage everything
    c. Focus on the church's mission
3. Ruling elders, as the end of their term approaches,
    a. Resign before their term ends
    b. Joyously exclaim "I'm glad that's over!"
    c. Are sad they will no longer be serving as elder
4. When our church asks people to serve as ruling elders and deacons, we
    a. Have to beg people to accept
    b. Have to recruit new members who don't know what they are getting in to
    c. Have people wanting to serve as elders and deacons
5. In our church, regular session meetings
    a. Are much too long
    b. Are tedious and a waste of time
    c. Energize participants who look forward to attending
6. Following session meetings, the parking lot is
    a. Filled with small meetings discussing what should have happened
    b. Filled with warm greetings and farewells
    c. Quickly emptied
7. In our session meetings
    a. We do not have any conflicts
    b. We often get into heated struggles
    c. We deal with conflicts in healthy ways
8. When a committee brings a report to the session, the session
    a. Often makes corrections or overrules the committee
    b. Sends the work back to the committee for reconsideration
    c. Is grateful for the fine work the committee has done
9. Our ruling elders and deacons
    a. Give and give until they burn themselves out
    b. Give and give, occasionally getting a little something back
    c. Receive as much as or more than they are giving

The Bible Tells Me So

For each of these statements about the Bible, indicate your position using the following scale:
1=Strongly Agree; **2**=Agree; **3**=Not Sure or No Opinion; **4**=Disagree; **5**=Strongly Disagree

(Note: you can change your responses at any time during the sharing of your responses.)

You	Statement
	1. God dictated the words of Scripture to the original authors who recorded them without addition or omission.
	2. God inspired the authors of Scripture in such a way as to ensure their writing, shaped by the author's individuality, nevertheless accurately recorded God's Word.
	3. God used the authors of the Scripture, in their own particular historical and cultural contexts, to communicate God's Word for that time and place.
	4. God has protected the translations of Scripture through the ages so that what we have in our modern Bibles is the same as God's original Words.
	5. The Bible is inerrant—completely without error of any kind.
	6. The Bible may contain errors and inconsistencies, but only in trivial matters.
	7. Apparent errors in the Bible are a result of our limited understanding of God's Word.
	8. The Bible is a human document. As such it is limited and is subject to errors of both fact and history.
	9. The Bible contains errors and inconsistencies, but that does not reduce its capacity to communicate truth.
	10. The Bible is a collection of interesting myths, stories, and tales—just like other historical writings—that conveys important truths to every age.
	11. Modern knowledge and experience may override biblical understandings and invalidate what the Bible says.
	12. The Bible contains everything there is to know about God.

The Church and Authorities

For each of the following situations, in the corresponding column, choose up to **five** authorities a person *should* or *could* turn to in deciding on a response to the situation. Then, rank each of your choices in order of importance (**1=most** authoritative, **5=least** authoritative). The question of whether or not to tithe is filled in for you as an example (column e.g.)

Column Decision

    e.g. Whether or not to tithe.

      A Whether an adult, baptized as an infant, should be allowed to be re-baptized after a life-changing experience.

      B Whether a church should keep a pastor who gets a divorce while serving that congregation.

      C Whether the theory of evolution should be taught in your public schools.

e.g.	A	B	C	Authorities
1				The Bible
				The life and teachings of Jesus Christ
				Historical teachings and doctrines of the Church
				Modern denominational position statements and declarations
3				The preaching/teaching of my pastor
				Recognized scholars in the Church
				Best-selling religious writers
				Denominational publications/curricula
				Non-denominational religious publications
				Church school teachers
4				Parental values
5				Opinions of peers and friends
				Community values
				Common sense
				Intuition
				Modern understandings of psychology
				Modern science
2				Personal prayer and seeking God's will
				Corporate discernment of God's will
				(add your own):

Alternate Small Group Exercises

If your leader assigns one of these, complete the worksheet individually and bring to share in your small group.

My Models of Faith

In column I, write the names of persons who have been models of faith for you. List the most significant according to the prescribed age category. In column II, briefly explain why you consider that person a model of faith. In column III, list the characteristics you have "adopted" from your model. What did you take from them? Also list what you did not take in the process of establishing your own faith.

Ages	Column I Models of Faith: Name Individuals	Column II Explain Why Each Person Is a Model	Column IIIa What I "Adopted" from Models	Column IIIb What I Did Not "Adopt" from Models
CHILDHOOD Birth–14				
YOUTH 14–20				

Ages	Column I Models of Faith: Name Individuals	Column II Explain Why Each Person Is a Model	Column IIIa What I "Adopted" from Models	Column IIIb What I Did Not "Adopt" from Models
EARLY ADULT 20–35				
MIDDLE ADULT 35–55				
LATER ADULT 55 +				

My Faith Inventory

1. My first recollection of being in church is . . .

_____

_____

_____

_____

2. I was baptized in the _____ Church by
_____ when I was _____ years old.

3. The closest I have ever felt to God in my life was . . .

_____

_____

_____

_____

4. The time I have felt the greatest doubt or distance from God was . . .

_____

_____

_____

_____

5. Just before I die want to be able to say . . .

_____

_____

_____

_____

My Reflections and Goals for Faith Development

This worksheet will guide you in setting some personal goals in further developing your faith, which will in turn enhance the ministry of this church. Please prayerfully consider your responses.

1. This course has made me aware of . . .

_____

_____

_____

_____

_____

2. As a ruling elder/deacon, I feel a need to . . .

_____

_____

_____

_____

3. I would love to see our church . . .

_____

_____

_____

_____

_____

4. I need to deepen my commitment by . . .

_____

_____

_____

_____

_____

5. What I appreciate about time in small group was . . .

_____

_____

_____

_____

6. I need to grow in . . .

_____

_____

_____

_____

7. A goal I am setting for myself in my walk with Christ is . . .

_____

_____

_____

Anything else you would like to share with the group?

_____

_____

_____

_____

Please close the meeting with prayer together.

Case Studies

Case Study 2: Baptism, Pastoral Sensitivity, and Polity

Mike and Tara chatted excitedly as they rode with Rev. Billingsly to the Alexander home. This was a first for Mike, having an official role at a baptism. His election as a deacon in the Christ Covenant Presbyterian Church two years ago was one of the high points of his religious life. But it was his long-time friendship with Carl Alexander that prompted the special request that he be one of the representatives of the congregation for this baptism. Mike had always seen baptisms done in the sanctuary and wasn't even aware that they could be done at someone's home.

Tara, who had over ten years of service as an elder at Christ Covenant, had explained it to him. Last Sunday, Sally and Carl Alexander had approached Rev. Billingsly after services. They had asked if he could do their son Benjamin's baptism at their home. Carl's mother, Mabel Alexander, a beloved matriarch of the church, had spent the last five years homebound and bedridden. Her mind was sharp, and members who stopped by to see her always came away uplifted, but her body could no longer tolerate the rigors of getting to a worship service. Recent reports, sadly, had Mabel's conditioning worsening, and there were rumors of discussions with hospice. Mabel had her heart set on seeing Benjamin baptized and was the one suggesting a home baptism. Tara, as an elder, had assisted with many baptisms during worship but she, too, had not been to a private baptism. But Rev. Billingsly assured her this was proper as long as the congregation was well represented.

So, shortly before 2:00 p.m., on a beautiful Sunday afternoon, the contingent from Christ Covenant pulled up to the Alexander home. They were welcomed at the door and ushered into a spacious living room where at least twenty people were gathered. Mabel was in a day bed in one corner of the room being swarmed with greetings and hugs. Carl Alexander took Mike, Tara, and Rev. Billingsly into an adjoining room.

"We are so glad you're here," said Carl. "We are surrounded by family and friends, many of them from Christ Covenant, and mother is having a good day. Rev. Billingsly, I hate to spring this on you at the last minute, but we have two special requests. You know Lisa and Tom Carter from the church? We would like them to stand with us as Benjamin's godparents. And my brother, George, and his wife are here from California. They are members of a Presbyterian church there. Anyway, they have a ten-month old girl that hasn't been baptized, and we thought you could do both today." Before Rev. Billingsly could respond, Carl escorted him out of the room saying, "Come on, I'd like you to meet the rest of the family."

Mike looked at Tara, who had a troubled look on her face. He said, "I didn't know Presbyterians had godparents. Is that something new?" He went on, "Anyway, are we *allowed* to baptize a baby from another church?"

Tara thought for a moment and then responded, "No, Presbyterians have *something*, but it's not godparents. And, I *think* we can baptize children from another congregation." Right then Rev. Billingsly stepped back into the room and addressed Mike and Tara, "We need to talk!"

Discussion

1. What is at stake here, in terms of Presbyterian polity: theologically and pastorally?
2. What references from the Constitution apply to these issues? *Book of Order*? *Book of Confessions*?

3. If the folks from Christ Covenant Church were to follow a strict interpretation of polity, what would they do?
4. In this specific situation, can a case be made for a different approach/response? If so, what might that be?
5. If you were advising Rev. Billingsly, Mike, and Tara, what specific counsel would you give them?

Case Study 3: The Mission Budget

Linda Higgins rolled her eyes in disbelief.

This was only her third year as an elder in the Valley Springs Presbyterian Church, and she was still discovering all the ins and outs of how Presbyterians do things. Her parents had been lifelong Baptists, but after trying out a variety of churches in early adulthood, including a brief affiliation with the local Catholic parish, she decided the Presbyterians felt the most comfortable. It wasn't long after she joined the church that her interest in community outreach was noticed, and she was asked to serve on the Missions Committee. The next year she was nominated for and elected to serve on the session.

She found quite a few other folks in the congregation who shared her passion for missions beyond the church doors and soon became the acknowledged advocate for community outreach. Last year the Missions Committee had pushed for and accomplished an increase in mission giving from 12 percent of the overall church budget to 15 percent.

This year the Missions Committee, with Linda as the chair, decided to ask for an increase in the percentage going to outreach to 20 percent of the overall budget. Since anticipated increases in income would not cover this amount, some reordering of priorities would be needed. The extra funds were earmarked for two specific projects: an after-school tutoring program for at-risk elementary age children at which several church members, including one elder, served as volunteer tutors; and a feeding program for the homeless that, with this influx of money, could open its doors five days instead of only three days a week.

Knowing that this represented a major change in the church budget, Linda had worked closely with both the Board of Deacons and the session's Finance Committee to explain and interpret the Mission Committee's request. The Deacons were supportive. The primary resistance seemed to be from certain elders who were committed to repairing some annoying roof leaks in the Fellowship Hall and making much needed upgrades to the church's youth fellowship room.

The clerk of session had just counted the raised hands and announced the vote. What surprised and disappointed Linda was that the session voted 7 to 5 in favor of a budget that did *not* include an increase for missions. It seemed so unfair that a few persons had stood in the way of these important projects. So, as the session meeting drew to a close, she offered a motion. "Since our vote was so close, I move that we take the budget to the congregational meeting next month, give them the information we have heard here, and let them decide what the church's budget should look like. They're the ones who support the budget. They should have a say in how their money is spent." The motion was enthusiastically seconded, and the session began the debate.

Discussion

1. Do you think the session should approve this motion? Why or why not?
2. What is the issue here in terms of Presbyterian polity?
3. What principle(s) of Presbyterian government applies(y)?
4. What is at stake here in terms of Presbyterian theology? What belief(s) applies(y) to this situation? What references in the *Book of Order* inform your position?
5. What counsel would you offer to Linda?

Case Study 4: Left Behind in the Rapture

"We're really worried that the people we love are going to be left behind!"

The curriculum planning committee for the John Knox Adult Sunday School Class listened with polite interest. A small group from their class had, for months, been advocating a special series before the end of the year that would explain current world events and urge people to accept Christ before the second coming. Today they were making their case before the planning committee.

"There are members of our families—there are members of this church—who only look like Christians. They have never truly accepted Christ as their Savior and will be left behind at the time of the Rapture."

The chair of the planning committee interrupted. "Your passion for your beliefs is clear. But I'm confused. I've not heard this understanding of Scripture taught in our church in classes or from the pulpit. How did you come to these beliefs? And why should we use our class to present them?"

"You are right. We've been attending a weekly Bible study for years that explains the Scriptures in a way we don't hear in church. Sometimes I think the church is intentionally keeping people ignorant about these things. But this way makes a lot of sense. You may have read or seen one of the best-selling novels (they are in the inspirational fiction section of all the major book stores and have sold over 65 million copies) that try to get the message to the general public. Recently, a major independent motion picture tried to explain what's happening, but Hollywood ignored it—in spite of the fact that Hollywood has two movies showing right now that deal with the end of times and the battle we are in with Satan and all the evil in the world. Anyone who carefully reads the Scriptures can see that the end of the world is coming soon. We need to spend all our energy in getting ready."

"Well, I'm all for evangelism," said the committee chair, "but isn't this a little far out for us Presbyterians?"

"That's just the point! It's not far out. It's God's plan. In the Old Testament, God was a God of wrath that required obedience to the law for salvation. Since Jesus Christ entered the world, God is a God of love that saves us by grace through faith. But now, anyone who reads the newspapers can see that the prophesies of the Scriptures are coming true in our time. Before long, Christ will return again in the Great Rapture and take all true believers in the first resurrection, leaving behind everyone else. The ones left behind will have seven years of peace—halfway through, the anti-Christ will be revealed. But Christ and legions of angels will bind Satan for a thousand years of peace in the Kingdom Age, after which the Devil will be released, only to be defeated in a final battle. Then the general resurrection will occur, the Final Judgment will take place, and we will begin eternity in the new heaven and earth. I want the people I care about to know these things and become true believers—taken up with Christ in the Rapture—not left behind. Please, let us bring this message to the class."

The committee sat in silence for quite a while until the chair spoke up. "Thank you very much for coming today. We will discuss your request and get back to you."

After the folks left, the committee continued in silence for a moment until everyone began talking at once . . .

"Is this Presbyterian theology?"

"I've read two of those left-behind books, and they are really good!"

"Has anyone else seen that movie with what's-his-name in it?"

"Does anyone believe this stuff?"

"Have you heard any of this before?"

"What is our church's teaching on the end of times?"

"Some of this make sense to me."

"Do you think our class wants to hear this?"

"Okay, people, settle down," said the chair. "Let's figure out what we are going to do. While this topic is not very clear to me, I don't see any reason why we can't offer it to our class—there sure seems to be a lot of interest in it."

One of the committee members interjected, "Isn't the session supposed to approve the education program of the church? This may be controversial. Shouldn't we get their approval?"

Another member spoke up, "It's our class. Why does the session have to approve what we offer?"

Someone else said, "I'd really like to hear what our church believes about the Rapture."

The chair tried to bring an end to the discussion. "Here's what I suggest. The session is meeting next week. During the announcement time, I'll tell the session about our member's concerns and our offering a series of classes on the topic and see if anyone has an objection. How's that?"

The following week during the announcement period the report was made—but the reaction of the session was anything but benign. A lengthy discussion followed.

Discussion

1. If you were on the session, how would you have reacted to the announcement?
2. What is the issue here in terms of Presbyterian polity?
3. What principle(s) of Presbyterian government applies(y)?
4. What references in the *Book of Order* inform your position?
5. What is at stake here in terms of Presbyterian theology?
6. What belief(s) applies(y) to this situation?
7. What portions of the *Book of Confessions* inform your position?
8. Where would you go to get more information on this topic?
9. What do you think is the church's responsibility in dealing with this topic?
10. What course of action would you recommend?

Case Study 5: Member, Member, Who's a Member?

John Ardor was glad this was the final meeting of his task force. He chided himself for speaking up last summer, but he felt strongly about the issue. He figured, "I've never done this before, but how hard can it be?"

For several years, the Zwingli Memorial Presbyterian Church had been on hold, but now with their new pastor about to arrive, things were really beginning to take off again. The Rev. Sam Hampton wasn't even in place, yet already the church was feeling an excitement that many had thought was long gone. For years, ZMPC had hovered around one thousand members on the rolls. But worship attendance recently was only in the upper two hundreds. The rolls had not been reviewed in more than five years, and everyone knew the real active membership of the church was much less than a thousand. Just this year, the new treasurer announced she had discovered ZMPC was paying a denominational per-capita for every active member reported in the church's annual statistical report. This fact, and the impending arrival of the new pastor, had rekindled in John a desire to bring the church's membership rolls up to date. When he said as much in last summer's session meeting, in true Presbyterian fashion, he was asked to convene a task force to review the rolls and report back to the session by November—prior to the nominations for next year's church leaders in ordered ministry. Both elders and deacons were appointed to the task force. Most of the task force members were long-time members themselves who, between them, knew almost everyone on the rolls in person.

John had called his task force together twice before. In these two meetings they had carefully reviewed the rolls and took the following actions:

- Immediately deleted from the active membership sixty-five people who had moved out of town in the past five years
- Deleted thirty-one people who had not made a financial gift to the church in over three years
- Removed twelve persons from the active rolls who were deceased
- Deleted one college student who was attending school in another state and whose parents had also moved to another state
- Removed seventeen people who had requested transfers to another church
- Removed six people who someone knew had joined another church in the area
- Removed thirty-four people from the active rolls who had two years ago resigned en-masse, upset over a problem with the former pastor

Tonight, the task force was going to wrap up their work. They had two things left to do. Someone had suggested that the task force review the *Book of Order* to make sure they had covered all the bases; and they had to make decisions on three difficult cases:

- Sarah Purnell, a member for over thirty years, was bedridden in a nursing home, unable to attend worship or financially support the congregation
- Bob Markham, once a very active member, had a falling out with the church some years ago. For at least two years, Bob made a point of *not* attending worship and *not* giving to the church and letting his friends in the community know why. His negativity was a constant irritant to the revitalized church.
- Carter Samuelson joined the church just two years ago, but, as everyone knew, he had done so only because he was running in next year's mayoral election. Carter supported the

church generously but rarely came to worship. Many members had commented on how upset they were that he was using the church so obviously for his political purposes. Some had gone so far as to suggest that he be dropped from the rolls.

John called the task force to order. As he looked at the folks gathered around the table, he sensed he was in for a long evening—a lot of troubled and anxious faces were staring back at him.

"Well, let's get started and wrap this up. The Budget Committee has called me to see how much we are going to save next year in per-capita expenses. The Nominating Committee needs to put their slate together. And I promised myself we would have these rolls cleaned up before Sam arrives. What did you discover in your *Book of Order* research, and what are we going to do about our three special cases? Who wants to go first?"

There was silence for a moment, and then everyone tried to speak at once . . .

Discussion

1. In the *Book of Order*, what do you find about church membership and the review of rolls process?
2. Based on your understanding, what issues and concerns would you have brought to this meeting regarding:
3. the actions the task force had already taken?
4. the three special cases?
5. What is the issue here in terms of Presbyterian polity?
6. What principle(s) of Presbyterian government applies(y)?
7. What are the primary references in the *Book of Order* that inform your position?
8. What is at stake here in terms of Presbyterian theology (i.e., the meaning of church membership)?
9. What would you recommend the task force do at this point in time?

Case Study 6: Calvin Presbyterian Church

Bill Smith couldn't sit quietly anymore. In frustration, he jumped to his feet and said, "I move the previous question. It is time for the session to vote on this."

It all started eight years ago, when Bill joined Calvin Presbyterian Church. If it hadn't been for his wife, he might not have joined, but she wanted to be a part of a church as they raised their two kids. Bill had not gone to church as a child. In his youth, he had visited many churches with his girlfriends. After college and his marriage he began attending Calvin Church at the urging of his wife.

Much to his surprise, he found he really enjoyed the church and its people. Many of the members were folks just like him, and he even liked the pastor's sermons. It wasn't long before he agreed to serve on one committee then another. Bill discovered that folks appreciated what he did for the church and what he had to say.

As Bill got more involved in the church, he became aware of the larger denomination and found he didn't agree with many of the stands the PC(USA) took on a variety of social issues. When Bill spoke up in classes and other gatherings, many people supported his positions. Some even encouraged him to run for elder.

When the nominating committee approached him last year to serve a three-year term as an elder in the church, Bill was eager to accept. After a six-week training class, Bill was ordained and installed and began his active service on the session.

It wasn't long before Bill realized that the church looked and felt much different when viewed from the inside as opposed to what the regular members saw. While this concerned him, he took seriously his leadership as an elder.

In the weeks prior to the session meeting, word had come from the General Assembly about some controversial amendments to the Constitution of the church. These amendments were going to be presented and voted upon at an upcoming meeting of the presbytery. Through his circle of friends and acquaintances, Bill knew that these amendments were trouble waiting to happen. He felt very strongly that the church should take a stand against them. So when the session asked for volunteers to be commissioners at the presbytery meeting, Bill volunteered and was elected unanimously.

It was the session's debate on these issues that brought Bill's frustration to a head. Most of the session agreed with Bill's position, but there were some strong dissenting voices. When Bill called the question, the vote was taken. The session voted to reject the amendments by a two-vote majority. Bill rose again to speak. "I don't know why we waste our time on these issues. The church up there sends these controversial issues to us down here without a clue as to where the local congregations stand on these proposals. I think we should just ignore the denominational stuff from here on. Our church doesn't need all this trouble. I move we file all these matters in a folder and just ignore them!"

Discussion

1. Do you think the session should approve this motion? Why or why not?
2. What is the issue here in terms of Presbyterian polity?
3. What principle of Presbyterian government applies?
4. What is at stake here in terms of Presbyterian theology?
5. What belief(s) applies(y) to this situation?
6. What references in the *Book of Order* inform your position?

Case Study 7: Predestination

"Hey, B! You're a Presbyterian aren't you? Come here a minute."

B turned to the sound of that name being called in the crowded coffee shop. Part of the work ethic these days included a stop on the way to the office at the gourmet coffee shop for some liquid caffeine and a muffin—bran of course! Usually the mornings were spent in quiet reflection before the start of an inevitably hectic day. But today, B was drawn to a small table by the window where three folks were waving a welcome. Coffee and muffin in hand, B threaded through the crowd to the table.

"Morning, B. Cal from Rotary. This is Armen and Ian—some folks I work with. You're a Presbyterian—even a church leader—aren't you?"

"Yes," said B suspiciously, trying to remember if the denomination had been in the news recently. "What's going on?"

"We've been having a discussion since Marti's funeral last week. Did you know her?"

"Just by reputation. She died in that horrible car accident on the interstate, didn't she?" replied B.

"Tragic," said Cal. "She was driving home from work when a pipe fell out of a truck, bounced off the roadway, and crashed into her windshield, killing her instantly—had a husband and two young children. Anyway, Armen was at the funeral, and the pastor talked about Marti being predestined and safe in God's hands. We all knew Marti, and she wasn't what you would call—how can I say this—a religious person. Now, me . . . I believe when your time comes, you're going to die, no matter what you're doing or who you're with. When your time is up, it's up, and there's nothing you can do about it. Armen here, believes that anyone who hasn't stood up and professed their faith before they die will go to . . . you know, down there. Then Ian is telling us about this predestination thing. Ian, ask B your question."

Ian spoke, "Well, I've always been taught that one of the basic beliefs of Presbyterians was predestination—where God has already chosen some people to go to heaven and some people to go to hell. And since God has already chosen which is which, there's nothing that you can do about it. End of discussion. Isn't that what Presbyterians believe?"

Armen chimed in, "If Presbyterians believe that, then that makes God kind of capricious. What motivation would anyone have for making Jesus Christ their personal savior?"

Cal interrupted, "I thought predestination meant that God has already laid out the course of everyone's life—you know, fate—where everything that happens, even your time of death, is according to God's plan. So tell us B, what's the deal here on this predestination thing?"

B's mind was racing in circles thinking, "Where's a clergyperson when you need them? I've got to say something . . ."

Discussion

1. What response could B give that would be faithful to the Presbyterian understanding of predestination?
2. What is at stake here, or what is the issue in terms of Presbyterian theology?
3. What belief(s) and doctrine(s) apply to this situation?
4. What references in the *Book of Confessions* inform your position?

Case Study 8: Charlotte, Worship, and the Body of Christ

As moderator of the deacons for the past two years, Gloria had heard from a number of disgruntled church members. When the deacons assumed responsibility for coordinating the ushers for Sunday worship, no one anticipated having to deal with this issue. But she was learning fast. Her instincts told her that this meeting with "representatives" from the congregation was not going to be easy. For several months there had been rumblings of discontent and now, a formal meeting. She prayed a silent prayer for guidance as five members of the congregation took seats in the conference room. After an opening prayer, Gloria began.

"Thank you all for coming. I'm here to listen to what you have to say."

"I guess I better start," said Bob Samuels, a thirty-year member of the congregation.

"Gloria, we appreciate you meeting with us. I think you know these folks: Carl—he's been a member almost as long as I have; Susan—has children and grandchildren involved with the church; Paul—joined about five years ago and was an usher in his former church; and Betty—one of our young singles whose parents are members. I guess you have heard talk in the church. We are here to ask for your help."

Bob continued, "The situation on Sunday mornings has gotten so bad that some folks don't want to come to church. Of course, we are taking about Charlotte Spencer."

Gloria said nothing, so Bob went on, "We all care about her, but things have gotten out of hand. This past Sunday was too much. We all had gotten used to the idea of having her in worship. Last year we even took out a section of a pew to accommodate her wheelchair. We have had speakers in our education program on Down's Syndrome to help us understand what's going on. Bless her heart! Her mother, Joanne, has her hands full! It's enough caring for a normal teenager, but she can barely control her daughter. It is distracting enough when Charlotte whoops along with the singing of the hymns, but when she started responding to Rev. Knox in the middle of his sermon, I thought people were going to walk out."

Gloria interjected, "I thought Rev. Knox handled the situation gracefully."

"But he shouldn't have to handle anything!" said Susan. "When we come to worship we want to do just that and not have to listen to all these distractions. Why can't she have her own church just for her? I don't know how much longer my family can tolerate this."

Carl spoke up, "We want the ushers to ask the mother to do *something*—either get her child under control or don't bring her to worship."

Paul looked pained as Betty joined in, "So what are you going to do?"

Discussion

1. If you were Gloria, what would you say or do: at this moment? in the weeks to come?
2. What is at stake here in terms of Presbyterian polity and theology?
3. What references in the *Constitution* inform your reflection and guide your practice?

Case Study 9: Believe It or Not

Stan hung up and knew he was in trouble. The phone call from Steve and Sally was a surprise, and he could tell they were very upset. They had a bad experience in their first Sunday school class this morning. They just couldn't believe what they had heard, and they had some hard questions.

Two months ago, Sally and Steve joined Pilgrim Presbyterian Church because it was convenient to their new home and, of all the churches they had visited in the last year since their move into the area, it had the best childcare facilities and program for their three-year-old daughter.

Both had grown up in small towns and, although they had not attended church much as children and youths, they had started attending a non-denominational chapel shortly after their marriage. The pastor there was quite a powerful preacher and didn't mind telling folks what they should believe—which, as novices to the Christian faith, they found comforting. They had gotten involved in a young adult Sunday school class there and discovered they enjoyed studying and learning about the Scriptures.

Which was why, when they moved, they wanted to attend a Sunday school class at their new church. This was their first Sunday attending the Young Adult class at Pilgrim Presbyterian.

They just couldn't believe what they heard. One of the class members, apparently a regular teacher of the class, made a presentation on "What Everyone Should Know about the Bible." He proceeded to say that the world *wasn't* created in seven days, Adam and Eve were *not* real people, Moses *didn't* write the Torah (the first five books of the Old Testament), David *didn't* write all the Psalms, the prophets were *not* predicting the future, the Gospels were *not* *real* history, many of Jesus' sayings were *made up*, and Revelation was *not* about the future. Amazingly, even though some class members pushed the teacher on several points, most people in the class were not troubled at all by what he had to say.

Sally and Steve were shocked. Everything they had learned about the Bible told them the Bible was true—just as it was—and that people messed around with the Bible at their eternal peril. They had heard their previous pastor talk about how God had inspired the writing of the Bible and had protected every word from error. Their growing faith was built on the solid assurance that everything they read in the Bible was true—absolutely true. And here was a person—perhaps a whole group of people—who were saying just the opposite.

On their way home after the class, they agreed if this was what Presbyterians really believed, they were out of here. Yet they really liked the people and had made some friends at this church. Since Stan had befriended them when they first arrived and happened to be one of the church's ruling elders, Sally suggested they give him a call when they got home.

Stan had listened carefully and, realizing he needed a well-prepared response, suggested they meet the next evening after dinner to talk. What *do* Presbyterians believe about the Bible and *why*? Stan began to collect his thoughts and offered a quick prayer for guidance.

Discussion

1. If you were Stan, what are some of the things you would say to Steve and Sally?
2. What references or statements in the *Book of Confessions* or the *Book of Order* are applicable?
3. What is the official Presbyterian stance on the nature and authority of Scripture?

4. What is at stake in this situation in terms of Presbyterian theology? Presbyterian polity?
5. Are there some statements, stories, or beliefs from the Scriptures that are, for you, non-debatable?
6. If there are parts of Scripture that are not literally true, where does its authority come from?

Case Study 10: Baptizing Baby Bobby

"What do you mean you won't baptize baby Bobby?"

The intensity of Helen Jones' challenge to Rev. Knox would have scorched him in a face-to-face conversation; the several miles of telephone circuit between them was the only saving factor in this situation. She kept going.

"I can't believe the church refuses to baptize my grandson. We have been members here for over thirty years. My husband and I have served as leaders and worked on all kinds of committees. *And* we pledge to the church, a *substantial* pledge, I might add. When my son told me that you refused to baptize Bobby, it was too much. The child is already over a year old *and* we have already invited our family—coming from all over at considerable expense—to be here specifically for the baptism. And now you tell me it's not going to happen? I have a good mind to march my family right out of here and find a church that knows how to treat its members. What have we ever done to deserve this?"

"Helen," said Rev. Knox, "it's clear that you are upset. But I would like to explain if I could."

"I can't imagine any explanation that will help."

Rev. Knox took a deep breath and began, "Helen, when your daughter-in-law called the office and spoke to me, I didn't know they were part of your family. When she told me her name, I looked in the member list and couldn't find them. Neither of the parents are active members here, or anywhere else, from what she told me."

Helen interrupted, "But Bob grew up in the church and did come to Sunday school regularly until he was a teenager. Something happened in middle school, though, that turned him off from the church, and we couldn't even get him to go through the confirmation class. After that he just drifted away from the church. He and his wife were married here five years ago, and we have tried to get them to come, but you know how young adults are these days. I know he is not as active as he should be, but that shouldn't make Bobby ineligible to be baptized."

"Helen . . ." began Rev. Knox, but Helen broke in.

"Are you going to baptize Bobby or not?"

"I'm sorry, Helen," said the Reverend, "I can't."

"Well, we'll just see about that. Maybe the session will have something to say about that. Good-bye, *Reverend*." And with that parting remark, Helen hung up.

As soon as Helen hung up, she dialed a new number. It is your phone ringing. You answer, and she begins her story . . .

Discussion

1. Was the pastor correct in refusing to baptize this child?
2. Who, according to the Constitution, is entitled to present their child(ren) for baptism?
3. What understandings of baptism as a sacrament and as a theological act are especially important in this situation?
4. What are some of the ways that the session and the pastor can respond to this situation in a pastoral, and not just legalistic, way?

Case Study 11: Meetings, Committees, and the Presbyterian Way

"If you are available and would be willing to be a commissioner to the presbytery meeting on the tenth, raise your hand . . . Nobody? Remember, we are entitled to three commissioners. Last meeting, I was the only representative from this church. Well, give some thought to it and let me know if you can attend."

Frank Jones, as moderator of the session, was frustrated. For the last several years, it seemed no one wanted to go to the presbytery meetings. He had tried assigning folks to specific meetings, but something always seemed to come up to prevent them from attending. He tried to wrap up the meeting.

"Okay. That's all of the business for this month. Don't forget: Budget Committee meets Thursday at 7:00 p.m.; Education Committee meets next Monday at 7:30; Outreach Committee meets next Tuesday afternoon at 5:00; all committee chairs meet a week from Wednesday at 7:30; and the Kitchen Committee meets a week from Sunday at noon following worship. Anything else? Then let us stand and be adjourned till next month. Let us pray . . ."

In the parking lot following the meeting, Stan, Mike, and Carol stopped to chat (as they often did) before they went home.

Stan, who had become an elder just two years ago, expressed his frustration.

"I know Frank is frustrated about not having commissioners for the presbytery meeting, but I have to tell you, I signed up to go my first year on the session, figuring it was something that elders are supposed to do. Boy, was that a waste of time! First we drove almost ninety minutes to get to this church across the county, and then we sat all day. It was one of the most boring things I have ever done—people giving reports, voting on stuff I had no clue about, and arguing about things that no one cares about."

"Well, I've never been to a presbytery meeting," said Carol, "but all these committee meetings at church are killing me. It seems like all we do is meet in committees. Every time something new comes up, the first thing we do is create a committee. We meet and meet, and it takes forever for anything to be decided. Sometimes I wonder if we shouldn't just let the pastor make the important decisions—just so we can get on with it."

"You know," joined Mike, "that in the beginning of creation, a committee was assigned to create a horse—the result was a camel! Why are Presbyterians so enamored by committees and presbyteries when they are so inefficient?"

Discussion

1. Why do you think Presbyterians spend so much energy in committees and in deliberation?
2. What passages in the *Book of Order* provide an insight into the Presbyterian penchant for committees and deliberative assemblies (e.g., presbytery meetings)?
3. Can you think of any stories from the Scriptures that shed light on this Presbyterian practice?
4. What church leaders can serve as commissioners to a presbytery meeting?
5. How many commissioners is a congregation allowed to send to presbytery?
6. What vow, taken during ordination, is related to attendance at presbytery meetings?
7. What suggestions do you have that might make serving as a presbytery commissioner more fulfilling? Serving on church committees more satisfying?

Case Study 12: Church Membership—Easy or Hard?

After a brief opening prayer, the Evangelism Committee of Witherspoon Presbyterian Church began their monthly meeting.

Lou, chair for the past two years, began with a report on the new members' class. "Folks, we've had another good month. In this class, we took in eight people. That makes twenty-four for this year, and we still have three months to go. We seem to be doing a pretty good job of keeping in touch with our visitors and encouraging them to become members here. As we all know, there's a lot of work that still needs to be done getting our members connected with some aspect of the church other than worship and keeping them involved. Nevertheless, we seem to be offering what people are looking for in a church. If this net gain keeps up, we are going to have to add another worship service and seriously consider an expansion to our facilities—wonderful "problems" to have! Thanks to all of you for your calls, visits, and follow-up with the prospective members."

"As you may remember from last month's meeting, we agreed to give Claire some time at this meeting to report on her visit to a church in Washington. Claire, you're on."

Claire had been a member of Witherspoon Church for the last six years. She had grown up in a strict, non-denominational church in a nearby town. After the typical hiatus in her late teens and twenties, Claire started to attend Witherspoon Church soon after her first child was born. Her involvement in the church seemed to grow each year, and her passion for Christian discipleship in all areas of life was well known and respected. She addressed the committee.

"I want to tell you about a wonderful experience I had recently. On a recent business trip to Washington, D.C., one of my colleagues suggested that I might enjoy visiting a church there. It is called the Church of the Disciples and has about the same number of members as we do. They have a fantastic education program both on Sundays and during the week for adults, youth, and children. They have literally hundreds of outreach opportunities to choose from and sponsor support groups and community organizations every night of the week. They have multiple, full worship services every Sunday. What I really liked was their emphasis on discipleship—putting faith into action. What I found absolutely amazing, though, is that they have a two-and-a-half-year-long waiting list for church membership! Quite some time ago, they made the decision that their membership size was just right and that they really didn't want to grow any bigger. They decided to take church membership very seriously. You have to attend for six months before you can even apply for membership. Then, you have to complete two years of course work in the areas of Bible, theology, and Christian discipleship. During that time, you have to commit to regular worship attendance, plus regular involvement in some outreach ministry. Once you have finished all the preliminary requirements, you can join at one of the two services yearly at which time *all* the members of the church also have to reaffirm publicly their commitment."

"Anyway, it got me thinking. Why don't we demand more here for church membership? It's like we take *anyone* who walks in the door for *whatever* reason. I'm convinced a lot of people just want their names on the roll and could care less about being a disciple. Imaging what this church would be like if we raised the bar of membership to take in only folks who were really serious about participating in God's work! I think we should look into it."

Several committee members started talking at once.

Lou called for order and, when he had everyone's attention, asked, "Did anyone bring a *Book of Order*?"

Discussion

1. What are your thoughts on raising the expectations for membership?
2. What is at issue here? What might be some benefits of this plan? What might be some burdens?
3. What are the minimum qualifications for membership in the Presbyterian Church? How strict *can* they be?
4. What, if any, are the responsibilities of membership in a PC(USA) congregation?
5. What are some of the theological issues connected with high (and low) expectations for membership?

Case Study 13: What Age Communion?

Joan gasped as the half-filled glass of purple grape juice spilled on the floor. "Oh, for heaven's sake!" she muttered. (A good Presbyterian imprecation, by the way.) She grabbed the little glass as it slipped from her hand and dropped it into the plastic bag with all the others. Someday, she thought, someone will invent a better way to do this. She looked across the pews and saw her friend, Carol, watching with a bemused smile on her face. "Don't start," Joan warned. "Let's get this done and get some lunch."

Over the next ten minutes, Joan and Carol gathered all the communion glasses from their side of the sanctuary and walked together to the sacristy. Their fellow leaders, Kurt and Doug, were already dumping their load of glasses into the trays destined for the dishwasher. As they entered the room, Doug called out, "Hey Joan, want us to put bigger glasses on your side next month?"

"Very funny, Doug." Joan pause for a moment, then continued. "Have any of you noticed the Barclay family that sits on my side up near the front? The parents are here almost every week, but on the first Sunday they bring their kids to worship and give them Communion. What bothers me is that these kids couldn't be more than five or six years old. They probably look forward to a little snack every month in church. When I was growing up, I had to wait until I was confirmed before I could take Communion. You'd think the parents would have enough sense to teach kids the proper respect for the sacrament!"

"When I was a child," began Kurt, "I had to memorize and recite the catechism before I could take my first Communion. Seems to me that was before confirmation, but that was in the Catholic Church. I must have missed that class in leader training because I can't remember what Presbyterians are supposed to do."

Carol joined in. "I think you do have to take a class when you get into Junior High School before you can take Communion. Isn't it part of the confirmation training?"

"It must be," said Kurt. "It's been almost fifteen years since my son went through Presbyterian confirmation, but I remember his having to wait until then before he could participate in Communion."

Joan responded. "I think it is wrong for children so young to participate in the sacrament when they don't have a clue as to what it means. Maybe we could put a note in the bulletin with an age limit for participation . . . it just doesn't seem right to me."

"If you feel strongly about it," replied Doug, "then bring your suggestion to the next meeting of the session. No. Wait. You probably should let the Worship Committee know before you do that. They're the ones that handle Communion, and I think they can set the rules."

"You know," said Joan thoughtfully, "I just may do that."

Discussion

1. How old do you have to be in a Presbyterian church in order to take Communion?
2. What requirements have to be met before a person can take Communion?
3. What is the role of the parents in this? The role of the session?
4. How has the Presbyterian understanding of children taking Communion changed in your lifetime?
5. What theological issue(s) is(are) at stake here?
6. What references in the *Book of Order* and/or the *Book of Confessions* inform your understanding?
7. What is the actual pattern or procedure followed at your church to prepare children to participate in the sacrament of Communion?

Case Study 14: Christians and Jews

"Madam Clerk," said Frank, moderator of session and twelve-year pastor of Faith Presbyterian Church, "I believe you have a request from the Board of Deacons."

"Yes, Mr. Moderator, I do." Janet, a life-long member of Faith Church, picked up a single sheet of paper from the table and said, "The Board of Deacons, at their last meeting, received a request for the use of our church facilities and, after much discussion, is sending it to the session for approval."

"Their recommendation is this: That the Faith Presbyterian Church invite the congregation of Kol Ami to use our Fellowship Hall for worship and education programs on Friday nights and Saturday mornings, beginning as soon as possible and lasting until the construction of their synagogue is completed—possibly another nine months to a year from now. That is the request, Mr. Moderator. If I may, I have some additional information."

"The motion is before us." Rev. Johnson stated. "Please continue."

The clerk continued. "Some of you may know that Kol Ami is a newly formed congregation in our area in the Reformed Jewish tradition. You may also know that Beth, one of our deacons, is married to Simon, who happens to be the president of the Kol Ami congregation. Kol Ami, up until now, has been meeting in the high school auditorium, but the school is adding an adult education program on weekends that needs the space—thus the need for a new, temporary site. I've checked the church calendar and, with a few exceptions that I'm sure can be worked out, this is workable."

The moderator looked at the room of elders and spoke, "The issue is before us. Is there any discussion before we vote?"

The room was quiet for a while until, after a suitable wait, the moderator continued, "If there is no discussion, all in favor . . ."

At that moment, Tom Moore spoke up from the rear of the room. "I really hate to bring this up, but I feel I must. I guess most of us knew this was coming to the session tonight. I, for one, have given it a lot of thought. I serve on the Evangelism Committee, and we have been wrestling with what it means to fulfill the Great Commission. As Presbyterians, we are pretty wimpy when it comes to sharing our faith with others. I wonder if we shouldn't be reaching out to our Jewish neighbors with our faith instead of offering them meeting space."

Karen Andrews spoke up. "Tom, I live next door to Beth and Simon, and I think the way they have raised their kids in both the Christian and Jewish tradition is a model of religious tolerance we can all learn from."

"As individuals," replied Tom, "we may appreciate what they do, but on some level I believe we should also be concerned with their salvation. If we care about their souls, we should be sharing the good news of Christ with them. Religious tolerance is one thing—but I think the church should draw the line at officially sanctioning a non-Christian religion. What would we do if a group of Muslims asked to meet here?"

At this, elders all over the room signaled to be recognized. The moderator allowed the discussion to continue for close to twenty minutes, during which time no clear consensus emerged. Finally, he stopped the discussion.

Discussion

1. What do you think the moderator should do to wrap up the discussion? To arrive at a response to the recommendation?
2. Would you have voted to let the Kol Ami congregation use the church facilities? Why, or why not?

3. Are there times, in your opinion, when religious tolerance is a way of avoiding the challenge of the Great Commission? What are some of the ways that evangelism and tolerance of other faith traditions collide?

4. What do you think the relationship should be between Christians and Jews? Christians and other non-Christian religions?

5. What references in Presbyterian constitutional documents are relevant to this discussion? Other reference materials?

Case Study 15: Pastoral or Polity?

When Margaret called last week, her voice cracked on several occasions, and twice she had to stop to regain her composure.

Karen was the pastor of the three-hundred-member Charity Presbyterian Church. In her fourth year as the pastor since graduating from seminary, Karen had grown to value and love this collection of God's people set in the suburbs of a growing city. The call from Margaret triggered all her pastoral alarms, but she had tried to listen carefully. When Margaret was able to convey her request, Karen was surprised that all she wanted was to meet with Karen and Jim, the clerk of session. Assuring Margaret that this would be no problem, Karen set up the meeting and couldn't help but wonder what this meeting was about. At the appointed time, there was knock at the door. Karen rose to greet Margaret and was surprised to see Carol Frazier with her. Both were invited in and had a seat.

Karen knew that Margaret and Carol shared a large, rambling home not too far from the church. She and many of the congregation had been there several times for delightful social occasions hosted by the two women. Margaret's term on the session expired last year. She had served on the Personnel Committee and was well respected for her leadership in the church. Carol was currently on the Board of Deacons and was in charge of the Meal-on-Wheels program.

Margaret spoke first. "Karen and Jim, thank you for seeing us. I have some bad news to share and a request to make." Margaret looked at Carol, who nodded, and continued. "Two weeks ago, we received some terrible news." Carol reached out and took Margaret's hand. "Carol has been diagnosed with terminal cancer. It's in her brain. They have given us— excuse me, her—about six months to live, with only a few months of independent living left."

Karen and Jim offered their condolences for a few minutes before Margaret went on. "Our request is this. You may or may not have known that Carol and I have been very close for the past fourteen years. Our relationship is more than just housemates." Carol spoke up for the first time. "We deeply love and care for each other. We have been content with few people knowing this. But suddenly, it seems very important to us to make what has been so real, more . . . ah . . . formal."

Margaret continued, "We would like to have a small ceremony with a few of our closest friends where we can affirm our love and commitment to each other and have you, Karen, as our pastor, marry us, or at least offer God's blessing, if you can. The reason we've asked Jim in on this is that Carol and I both know this may be awkward for you and the church. So, would you give it some thought and let us know if you can, in good conscience, do this? As you might suspect, we'd like to know sooner than later."

After Margaret and Carol left the office, Jim turned to Karen and said, "Okay . . . what do we do about this?" To which Karen responded, "That is exactly what I was going to ask you."

Discussion

1. What are the issues in this request? What are the potential blessings? The potential burdens?
2. To what extent is this a pastoral issue? To what extent is this a polity issue?
3. What references in our *Book of Order* provide guidance for the pastor and the clerk of session?
4. What references in our *Book of Confessions* help to understand the issues here?
5. Is there scriptural guidance that might shed some light on this matter?
6. If you were a leader in ordered ministry in this church, and the matter were brought to you for comment, what counsel would you give the pastor?

Case Study 16: In the Beginning . . .

Most of the agenda of the Christian Education Committee had been completed, and the chair, Maggie, was making a few announcements. To everyone's surprise, Clayton, one of the ruling elders serving on the committee, literally burst into the room. His entrance silenced the committee and, in a moment of embarrassed realization, Clayton apologized and sat down. It didn't take a psychic to realize that Clayton was highly agitated. As Maggie reminded folks of the next meeting, she started to adjourn.

"Maggie," interrupted Clayton, "I'm sorry to barge in on the meeting like this, and I don't want to keep people any longer than necessary, but could I please have a few minutes of the committee's time?" When no one objected, Clayton continued.

"You will not believe what I have been through before this meeting. I've just returned from our county Board of Education meeting—most of you know I teach tenth-grade science classes in our neighborhood high school. I, along with about twenty other science teachers, were invited to discuss the implications of a new state Board of Education ruling. I still can't believe our state board did this! They have ruled that all state science teachers now have to teach evolution as a *theory* (to use their words)—not as established science. We even heard rumors that next year a group of "religious leaders" will be lobbying the state board to require the teaching of *creation science* as a parallel theory to evolution. Good Lord! I thought we put this debate behind us in the 1920s with the Scopes trial. As a science teacher, I'm appalled at the thought of having to bring religion into the classroom. As a Presbyterian elder, I'm embarrassed to be connected in any way with the religious folks promoting this creationism baloney!"

"Now wait a minute, Clayton, that's pretty strong language." Sophie leaned forward in her seat and continued. "It has been years since I taught science in middle school, but I do know a few things. I've only been a member here for a couple of years, but my former church— Presbyterian—had a parochial school that went through middle school, and they believed in scientific creationism. I had always been taught evolution as the only truth. But I have to tell you, after listening to quite a few lectures and presentations by that school's faculty—all ordained ministers, by the way—I started to understand their concern. There is a lot of scientific evidence nowadays that challenges and even refutes the fundamental assumptions of evolution. They made a pretty persuasive case built on the Scriptures. And I know that a lot of people, myself as one of them, would rather believe in a world intentionally created by God than a world that just happened."

"All right," said Clayton, "how many on this committee believe that God created the world and human life literally in six days?" Four people raised their hands. "How many believe that humans evolved from lower forms of life?" The remaining five members of the committee raised their hands. After a moment of quiet, Clayton broke the silence. "Okay. Here's what I'm going to do. We are an education committee, and this is an education issue. I'd like to find out what our denomination says about this issue and docket some time at our next meeting to come up with a recommendation for the session. I think it's time to take a stand."

Discussion

1. In your opinion, is this issue a matter of concern for the Church? For schools? For whom?
2. What do you believe about the beginnings of the world?
3. What is the Presbyterian Church (U.S.A.)'s stance on this issue?
4. What confessional statements from the *Book of Confessions* speak to this issue?
5. Does the *Book of Order* have anything to say pertinent to this issue?

Case Study 17: The Will of God

The class began in attentive silence. Not a noise was made as Bob and Mary made their way to the front. To the extent it was possible to support their friends by the sheer intensity of their care and concern, the class surrounded the Livingstones with their love. And they waited.

Mary smiled and began first. "I can't tell you . . ." Her voice choked, and she paused to collect herself before going on. "We can't tell you how much your support has meant to us this past month. I don't think we could have survived without your love and our faith."

A little over a month before, the Livingstone's seventeen-year-old daughter, Susan, was driving to her high school. A driver changed lanes improperly and caused another driver to sideswipe a school bus. After hitting the school bus, that driver lost control of the car, crossed the centerline, and hit Susan's car head on.

Mary explained. "We know that nothing that happened was intentional as far as those drivers were concerned. There was no substance abuse, no road rage involved. Everyone makes mistakes when they're driving. So we don't have any ill will toward the other drivers."

Bill picked up the conversation. "We know, while people make mistakes, God doesn't. We would love to have Susan back, but knowing that her death was part of God's plan gives us a peace that quiets our grieving hearts. God intended for Susan to die that morning and we have to, as painful as it is, learn to trust in God."

Mary concluded. "We are not ready to face the whole church yet, so we will not be staying this morning. But we wanted our friends to know how much your prayers and support and our shared faith have meant to us. Thank you all and God bless you."

As Bob and Mary left, they accepted the class's expressions of love. Within a few minutes though, the class was quiet again. No one, it seemed, wanted to break the silence. Finally, Shelly spoke.

"My heart goes out to Bob and Mary. My daughter is in the same class at school as Susan, and we have been grieving with the Livingstones. But, and I hate to say this, I just can't accept that God *intended* for Susan to die. I know they have found some peace in this belief, but I don't think I could worship and pray to a God who would take the life of a seventeen-year-old girl."

Steven spoke up, "I admit that this kind of talk makes me uneasy, too. But isn't that what Presbyterians believe in—God's will? You have to admit, it sure seems to be a comfort to the Livingstones. But I just don't know . . . Deborah, you're one of our church leaders. What *do* Presbyterians believe? Is Susan's death the will of God?"

Discussion

1. What would you say to the class if you were in Deborah's place?
2. What *does* our Presbyterian faith teach about the will of God? Are we to accept all that happens as being part of God's plan?
3. What resources/references in the *Book of Order* or the *Book of Confessions* speak to this issue?
4. Under what, if any, circumstances would you raise these concerns with the Livingstones?
5. What is at stake here theologically? "Pastorally"—in the sense of expressing your care and compassion for others?
6. How have you, personally, sorted out the notion of God's will in the midst of tragic events?

Case Study 18: God Shed His Grace on Thee

The events of recent days were making everyone anxious. Responding to the terrorist attacks and the horrible loss of life, the church had provided extra worship services, and the whole community was pulling together in a way not seen in over fifty years. Worship attendance and patriotism were at an all-time high.

At the deacon's meeting the previous week, plans were made for supporting the families and individuals directly affected by the national tragedy. Donations were pouring in for relief efforts. The fact that First Presbyterian Church was located less than two hours from a major military base made everyone keenly aware of the very personal nature of the decisions being made by the government. Lots of prayers were being offered day and night. Rumors were flying that the local National Guard unit, which included a number of members of First Church, might be mobilized in the near future.

So it was only a small surprise that Sunday morning—as Beverly and John, deacons and ushers, greeted people in the narthex—Bob Marshall entered the narthex in full dress uniform, carrying an American flag. Actually, it was *Lieutenant Colonel* Marshall. Bob was one of the church family's native sons—having distinguished himself in Operation Desert Storm, winning several medals for bravery—and a frequent speaker at church programs. Beverly and John looked at each other across the entranceway as Bob approached John.

"Morning, John."

"Morning, Bob, you're looking real sharp this morning."

"John, I'll get right to the point. I've been talking to some of the church's veterans and other members, and we think it's a shame that we don't have an American flag in the sanctuary. Some people remember having one in the 50s and 60s, but not since then. So I bought this flag and a stand, and I'm prepared to march in front of the choir to place it in the front of the sanctuary. Where do you want me to put it?"

"Hang on for a couple minutes, Bob. I need to check on some things." John was immediately conflicted. He, himself, served a tour of duty during Viet Nam, and his brother was a former POW. So his patriotism was not in question. But he remembered clearly several discussions over the past week about the proper place of patriotism in a worship service. He hurriedly talked with Beverly, and they decided they needed some help.

Beverly saw the clerk of session walk in and quickly brought her up to date. But she was at a loss for suggestions. Just then, First Church's pastor, Alan Winters, entered the narthex followed by the choir. As the three leaders quickly filled him in on Bob's request, the organist began the processional music, and Bob, carrying proudly the American flag, stepped in front of the choir.

Discussion

1. Should Bob be allowed to process in with the flag? Why or why not?
2. Whose responsibility is it to decide this issue?
3. What are some positive benefits to having the flag displayed in worship? What are some negative burdens?
4. From a Presbyterian polity standpoint, is there any reason a flag should or should not be displayed?

5. From a confessional or theological standpoint, what are some of the issues at stake in this matter?
6. What creative solutions or responses to this awkward situation can you imagine?
7. What responses might the church leadership make in the following week?

Case Study 19: A Majority of Dissent

"Hey Sue . . . Dave . . . Hold up a minute." Phil called out to his friends as the worship service dismissed. "Do you have a minute? Step into my office, please." Phil directed Sue and Dave to a quiet spot away from the folks exiting the sanctuary.

It had been a rough year for Phil at Knox Memorial Presbyterian Church. In recent months, his frustration had reached a level that spilled out into more and more vocal and public critiques of how the church was being run and the decisions that were being made.

"What is it now, Phil?" asked Sue, grinning. "Session vote you down again?" Sue was a long-time member and ruling elder in the church. Her values and views were much like Phil's but she still liked to tease him.

"That's not funny, Sue, and yes, they did it again! Sorry *you* weren't at the meeting. Dave, have you heard what went on?"

Dave was relatively new to the church. This year was his first time serving as a church leader, and he was still trying to figure out this *Presbyterian* thing (with Phil's help). "Just the usual rumblings, Phil. What happened?"

"You know," said Phil, "sometimes I wonder how these people can call themselves Christians! They sure don't believe the same things I do. Last Wednesday night was the third time I had tried to open some minds on the session. Everyone here seems to be stuck in the 1950s. First, they rejected my motion to support a pro-choice position. Then they voted down a motion to overture the presbytery requiring them to invest their money in socially responsible institutions. Now, just this past Monday night, they shot down a motion to prohibit the use of Styrofoam anywhere in the church."

"Phil, I understand these things are important to you," said Sue. "But you are always coming up with these motions and springing them on the session. Do you even check to see if anyone else thinks it's a good idea before you bring the motion?"

"You are right! These things *are* important to me! In fact, I think one of the reasons I was elected to be a leader was to help change this church to be more open and responsible. And yes, I do talk to people before I make a motion. I know there are lots of folks in the congregation who support my ideas—but that stodgy session refuses to listen."

Dave jumped in. "I agree with you a lot of the time, Phil, but your ideas *are* heard and voted on—they just don't get much support. Can't you accept the fact that you tried, and then move on?"

"I know there are a lot of members that support me. I think I'll just round up a group of them and bring them all to the session meeting next month. Then maybe we can get some things done."

Sue frowned and paused, then said, "Hey, Phil, I'm not sure that's a good idea."

Discussion

1. What advice or council would you give to Phil?
2. What is at stake here in terms of polity? Theology? Civility? Doing things the *Presbyterian* way?
3. What are the proper ways to handle dissent as a church leader?
4. What if a person, in good conscience, *cannot* accept the way things are? What are their options as a church leader?
5. What references in the *Book of Order* and/or the *Book of Confessions* inform your thinking?

Case Study 20: Local Option

Sam Grant had watched the TV program with fascination and an increasing sense of unease. He was pleased to see such an evenhanded discussion of this controversial subject and proud of his friends, but he also knew this public exposure was going to affect his work at the church.

Sam had been a member of Peace Valley Presbyterian Church for almost fifty years. His mother and father had joined the church when he was in elementary school, and Sam couldn't imagine belonging to another church. Over the years he had become more and more involved in the church. This was his fifth term as a ruling elder, and four years ago he served as the church's first commissioner to a General Assembly. Sam loved the church and its people.

Working and living in the community brought him into daily contact with most of its members. So it wasn't much of a surprise to see Diane featured on this TV special. Diane usually kept a pretty low profile, but she was also known as a person of honor who stood up for what she believed. Sam had grown to like and respect her. She had been elected twice as ruling elder at Peace Valley PC and was well thought of by the members. It was through her efforts that the church began its ministry for battered women. Primarily through Diane's influence, money was raised, a home was purchased, a live-in staff was hired, and the church now maintained the community's only safe house for battered women and their children.

Most of the church membership knew that Diane lived with another woman, Frances Collins, also a member of the church—in fact, had lived with her for almost twenty years. Diane and Frances always helped at the church suppers and even sang in the choir. Diane never spoke publicly about her relationship with Frances, but Sam and most everyone he knew just assumed they were more than roommates. Apart from a few whispers here and there, the church embraced and appreciated both Diane and Frances.

Sam's dilemma was that, this year, he was chair of the church Nominating Committee and knew that Diane was once again being nominated as an elder at Peace Valley. The list of nominees had already been published, and the congregational meeting was this Sunday to elect leaders. Sam thought back to ten years ago when someone had raised a question about Diane serving as a church leader. Opinions varied, of course, but the overall consensus was that the Nominating Committee didn't want to explore or use sexual orientation or even sexual fidelity as a criterion for church ministry. (At least one current elder at that time would not have passed scrutiny, as later events confirmed.) In the nominating committee's judgment, *they* knew the people in their congregation and were confident in their ability to choose rightly. Yet Sam suspected, now that Diane and Frances had been identified as a lesbian couple on the TV special, they might have a problem.

Sam's concerns proved to be true when, two days after the TV special aired, he received a phone call from a member of the Nominating Committee asking him what they should do.

Discussion

1. How should this Nominating Committee proceed?
2. What is at stake here in terms of church polity? Theology?
3. Is being a practicing homosexual a barrier to ordination?
4. What are the current ordination/installation standards for leaders of the PC(USA)?
5. Would all the leaders of *your* congregation meet these standards?
6. In your opinion, how should local congregations choose their own leaders?

Case Study 21: The Presbyterian Way to Worship

"Sara, got a minute? Have you been to that new worship service?"

George caught up with his neighbor and fellow church member, Sara, who was heading out the door of the sanctuary on her way to her Sunday school class.

"No, I haven't," replied Sara "and it's not likely I will. I don't understand why the church approved such a thing in the first place. I do know it's not for me."

"I heard they have over a hundred people in attendance and getting stronger," George explained. "All the publicity said it was for all ages, but I suspect it's the youth driving this train."

"I don't know about that," Sara responded. "My aunt, who is over eighty, has gone several times, and she seems to like it a lot. She say she likes the informality, and the music is much more lively that in our regular worship service. Plus she says she can read the words on the TV screen. You know they project the words to the songs and responses up on a big projection screen?"

"I did hear that," said George. "I also heard they have a band with drums and guitars. I'm sure that's to attract the youth crowd."

"My aunt says there's a lot of young adults and families attending in addition to several of her friends." Sara continued, "I guess some people just like that kind of thing. What I can't figure out is how we got so far away from the Presbyterian way to worship. I mean, don't we have a book that tells the ministers and musicians what worship is supposed to look like? Presbyterians have worshiped the same way for hundreds of years. My grandparents and parents worshiped that way, and it's good enough for me. Why should we change tradition now?"

George responded, "Well, you have to admit, more often than not, our worship is low on the excitement meter. But I agree with you. I don't understand how the session approved a service so different from Presbyterian worship. Hey! There's Maggie. She was at that big leader's meeting when the Worship Committee explained the new service. She's been an elder before and even served on the Worship Committee. I think she's a deacon now, but let's ask her."

George called Maggie over, and Sara began. "Maggie, George and I would like you to tell us how it is that the church approved this new worship service that's so un-Presbyterian."

Maggie smiled. This wasn't the first time she had been asked this question. She gathered her thoughts and began. . .

Discussion

1. If you were in Maggie's place, how would you have responded?
2. Is there such a thing as a *Presbyterian* way to worship? If so, how would you characterize it?
3. What references in the *Book of Order* or *Book of Confessions* have relevance in this matter?
4. How does our Constitution describe a Presbyterian way to worship?
5. What does our Constitution say about styles of music in worship? The use of media? The form of service?
6. Are there any limits as to the shape or form of worship in Presbyterian services? If so, what are they?
7. What, in the Presbyterian way, is the primary function/goal of worship?
8. For Presbyterians, how is that function/goal achieved?

Case Study 22: The Essential Tenets

"Do you sincerely receive and adopt the essential tenets of the Reformed faith as expressed in the confessions of our church as authentic and reliable expositions of what Scripture leads us to believe and do, and will you be instructed and led by those confessions as you lead the people of God?"

Karen thought back to the Sunday a little over ten year ago when she stood before the congregation of Emmanuel Presbyterian Church and responded, "I do" to this question. Her ordination to ordered ministry in the church was still one of the highpoints of her journey in faith. Over the last decade, her service as deacon and ruling elder in the congregation was a source of both fulfillment and frustration.

But today, she was filled with conflict and concern as to whether she could, in good conscience, continue as a leader in the Presbyterian Church.

Maybe if she hadn't signed up for that religion course at the community college . . . Maybe if she hadn't started reading books on theology. Maybe if she had kept her opinions to herself, she wouldn't be in so much distress. But, then again, maybe she would.

Trying to make sense of her faith had always been important to her. She never grew weary of asking questions and always tried to give good reasons for *why* she believed as she did. Over the years, she found herself more and more uneasy with things she used to take for granted—things she once thought were absolutely *essential* beliefs for Christians—things like the virgin birth.

The more she read the Scriptures and studied the history of the church, the more she believed that the virgin birth was a theological statement and not a biological fact. Her studies revealed that, in the gospels, only Matthew and Luke mention it—and only then in a passing reference with little detail. The rest of the New Testament is silent on the issue. Over time, Karen felt a settling and a deepening of her faith as she slowly surrendered belief in the virgin birth as a requirement to be a true Christian. Then she made the mistake of mentioning her new thinking in Sunday school.

Several members of the class challenged her during class; and one person, also a church leader, spoke with her afterward to say that Karen shouldn't continue as a leader if she couldn't believe in the essential tenets of the church.

Karen remembered the ordination question she answered many years ago and wondered if she had, in fact, crossed a line. She had a meeting scheduled tomorrow with the pastor to discuss the matter, but for now she reached for her *Book of Order* and *Book of Confessions*. She thought to herself, "I guess I'd better bone up on what the *essentials* are that I am supposed to believe."

Discussion

1. Do you think Karen should continue as a leader in the Presbyterian Church if she can't believe in the virgin birth?
2. What, for you, does it mean to "receive and adopt the essential tenets of the Reformed faith"?
3. What does our Constitution say about the content of these "essential tenets?"
4. Who, in our Presbyterian system of government, determines what the "essential tenets" are?
5. If a leader determines that they can no longer "receive and adopt the essential tenets of the Reformed faith," what is she or he bound to do?
6. Are there beliefs you once held that, for you, are no longer essential?

Sample Faith Statements and Stewardship Journeys

Faith Statement 1

I believe in the Triune God. I believe that God is the creator and sustainer of the universe. He is all powerful, all knowing, and ever present. I believe that I was created in God's image and nothing can separate me from the love of God. I believe that through His grace, my sins are forgiven. I cannot earn God's grace—it's a gift given freely.

I believe that God sent His son, Jesus Christ, to live on earth in human form. Jesus was human, yet he was perfect—living a life free of sin. Despite our imperfect and sinful nature, God loves us unconditionally. To show the extent of His love, God sacrificed His Son for the forgiveness of our sins. I believe that through Christ's resurrection we have been given the gift of eternal life.

I believe that before Jesus ascended into Heaven, he gave us the gift of His Holy Spirit. I believe that Spirit lives within me, gently influencing my beliefs and actions.

I believe that the Church is a place where people gather in God's name. I believe that the Holy Spirit unites church members (with various talents and abilities) to work together as a community to spread the good news of God's redeeming love in the world. The Church educates, equips, and nurtures its members for this mission work. The Church also provides an opportunity for believers to worship God, to be claimed by God in baptism, and to be forgiven by God through the Lord's Supper.

I believe that the Bible was written by humans and inspired by God and the Holy Spirit. The Bible teaches us about God and how He would like us to live our lives. It is the living word. I'm amazed that I can read a particular Bible verse at various times in my life, and each time it can have a different meaning—depending upon what's happening in my life. I believe that's the work of the Holy Spirit.

While I don't know yet what my calling is, I'd like to live my life in response to all the blessings I've received. One of my favorite hymns, "Here I am, Lord," comes to mind when thinking about my purpose or calling. In particular, the phrase "I will go, Lord, if you lead me" encourages me to trust God as I engage in the ministry to which I am called. I believe that God will equip me for the journey and will go before me, preparing the way.

Faith Statement 2

I believe in God as the creator of all things and that God continues to guide the world and universe, and will eternally.

I believe that God spoke His word through His only son, Jesus Christ, and that through Jesus Christ, His word has been interpreted. Through Jesus Christ, the world has been saved eternally from sin. I believe that Jesus Christ is and will always be the head of the church.

I believe that the Holy Spirit inspires those willing to be inspired and works through each and every person. The Holy Spirit guides us through prayer and through our daily lives. I believe that we cannot always tell when the Holy Spirit is working through us and will never fully be able to.

I believe that the Bible is the interpreted word of God through Jesus Christ and the people that he touched and that it is the only written word of God. However, I believe that the Bible is not the only way to receive God's word, and it should not be treated as such.

I believe in the church universal and accept that it is an imperfect state. I believe that the church should be an accepting and inclusive place, filled with diversity, for all of us are the children of God and equal in His eyes.

I believe that my mission is to help others understand their faith and bring prosperity to not only the Presbyterian Church, but to the church universal. As a Christian, I believe that my purpose is to guide others in my community and bring Scripture and faith to those who are willing to receive it.

Faith Statement 3

I like to illustrate my faith with this analogy: We, humans on earth, are all actors putting on a show for God, who is the audience. But of course, actors can't write scripts or give their best work without feedback, so we have "prompters." Prompters are those through whom the Holy Spirit moves most. These are the people who guide the world and lead it to peace and love as God and Jesus taught, whether this affects one person or the entire world. The best part is that all the actors and prompters are trying their hardest to bring joy and glory to the audience and not disappoint, but even if an actor forgets his or her line every once in a while, or the antagonist wins a small victory, the audience still loves the show and its actors. God loves us no matter what.

I believe in God. I believe God shows unending, everlasting, and unconditional love for all of creation and that "neither death, nor life, nor angels, nor rulers, nor things present, nor things to come, nor powers, nor height, nor depth, nor anything else in all creation, will be able to separate us from the love of God in Christ Jesus our Lord" (Romans 8:38–39). God created each of us to be individual yet equal despite gender, race, age, class, nationality, etc. I love God and everything God has given to us, but I also believe that it is okay to be angry or frustrated with God; and even if some of us give up on God, God won't give up on any of us.

I believe in Jesus Christ. I believe Jesus died on the cross, the ultimate humiliation, for us, so that our sins may be forgiven. I believe this was an amazing act of mercy and grace, which we as human sinners cannot dream of repeating. I believe Jesus saw past all differences and strengthened the weak around him in his time on earth, and I believe he continues to give strength to the weak today.

I believe the Holy Spirit moves through us and uses us to spread the Word of God and peace of Jesus Christ in ways we may not always notice or that we otherwise would not be capable of.

I believe the Bible is a collection of Jesus' teachings and God's Word to help us. I believe the Bible must be interpreted and studied to find God's meaning.

I believe the Church is called to help others in need, whether that need be food, clothes, or faith. I believe the Church is called to be a place of love and peace while spreading the Word of God. I believe the Church should welcome and nurture all people who love God and claim Jesus as their savior.

I truly believe with all my heart that God loves us all, and I know I've said this many times already, but I can't emphasize enough how powerful that truth is for me. God never stops loving us. I also believe that everyone has some part within them, no matter how small, that loves God. I believe we will never fully understand God's plan or God's will, and I believe we are not meant to truly understand, but we are meant to be continuously searching and growing in our faith.

Faith Statement 4

I believe in God, the Almighty and universal. God is the creator of all things, including those we cannot see and those we don't fully understand. I believe God created us to be flawed and imperfect, so that we may seek God's guidance and come to know God.

I believe in God's grace—a gift into which we are born and a blessing we receive continuously. God is always present.

I believe in God's timing and God's will for humanity and for the world.

I believe in Jesus Christ—that he was born fully human and fully God. I believe and I know he sacrificed his life for mine, to forgive my sins before they were even committed. He provides infinite wisdom through his teachings and gives faith to his followers.

I believe in the Holy Spirit—the invisible force that is the voice of God, enabling me to make choices, giving me words to pray, and the discipline to listen for God's message to me.

I believe in the Holy Scriptures, as God's word to me and to the world and as a source of knowledge, especially in uncertain times.

I believe in the Sacraments. Baptism binds me to Christ, knowing that this shared experience is an expression of faith in acknowledging Jesus as Lord and Savior. The Lord's Supper serves as an important reminder of Christ's death and resurrection and God's sacrifice for us.

I believe in our Church—a community of believers who uplift one another, teach and profess the faith, and serve God's children around the world. I believe that, as an ever-reforming church, we will adapt to changing needs and beliefs and that we will always be an inclusive community.

I believe in serving Christ by:

- Walking in faith and teaching that faith to others,
- Deepening my commitment to Christ and getting to know him better, and
- Serving my community as Jesus did.

I believe in the power of prayer, which is the truest affirmation of the presence of God.

Faith Statement 5

I believe . . .

That God's grace, even though I don't deserve it, is all sufficient for me.

That in response to this unconditional love first given by God, which God sealed for my sake through the life, death, and resurrection of His Son, Jesus Christ, I am called through faith, to share that good news with others by both word and deed.

That our one and only Triune God—Father, Son, and Holy Spirit—is Sovereign, a sovereignty I trust without hesitation or reservation.

That Jesus Christ is my personal Lord and Savior and also my constant companion through the Holy Spirit, who, like a close friend, will never give up on me no matter how often I may try to ignore or even deny him.

That as a disciple of Jesus Christ, I am also called to a different way of life—one that constantly seeks, in community with other believers, to discern the will of God for myself, God's church, and this world.

That because I have been richly blessed in so many ways, I must therefore use and share those God-given gifts in ways that hopefully will both honor God and be a blessing to others.

Stewardship Journey 1

I was taught to tithe. While I have never given ten percent of my income to a congregation, I have, at times, given more than a tithe away.

I have donated to the mix of faith-based organizations; community organizations that impact those in crisis or need; youth organizations; educational institutions; the arts and other groups who work to improve our community, state, or nation has varied. I have moved more to faith-based giving in the past few years.

If I give my time, I am motivated to give my money. The more I see of the church or any organization in action, the more I want to help financially.

Recently, I was challenged by the comments of a friend who observed, "I see giving, generosity, as a discipline that I must cultivate, an important lesson in my faith journey. My offering reflects my gratitude. It is a form of worship. It is recognition that everything is God's, and God has asked me to share only 10 percent of it. What happens to the money once I let go of it is not important. What is important is that I let go of it. What the group or people I give it to do with the money is between them and God."

To me this was a revolutionary idea. Shocking actually. I consider carefully which requests for gifts to respond to. It is against my nature not to want to know exactly what my gifts are used for.

But I have not been able to forget what my friend said. I consider wanting to know what happens with my dollars good stewardship. I will always believe that I should be discerning in selecting the recipients of gifts, but now I must also consider where discernment ends and where a need for control begins.

Is giving to the organizations I am active in really promoting my agenda and myself?

It's God's money, and God is in control—not me.

Stewardship Journey 2

It would be impossible, after twenty-six years of marriage, to separate my stewardship journey from my wife's. She regularly challenges my giving, and because of that I am more a generous and also a more discerning giver. It is a great blessing to see eye-to-eye with one's spouse in giving, one that I think is vastly underestimated, even in faith circles.

I grew up in a family that tithed and still does. For my parents, tithing meant ten percent of their earnings, which they spread among a few Christian ministries—including our church—and a couple of missionary programs. My parents were of modest means, and so I know that their giving was truly sacrificial—I lived it! Notwithstanding that commitment to God, my folks rarely made a forward commitment to church or to any other philanthropic group as far as I know. They grew up in an age and in places where money was scarce, and that experience stayed with them. While they always gave, I don't think that they ever developed enough trust in their circumstances to make forward commitments.

My wife and I have taken direction in our adult lives from great givers at this congregation. We also consulted Christian financial and estate-planning professionals, and so where we are today is our very personal take on those examples.

We think that the Bible is clear that God's minimum financial requirement of us is that we give ten percent of first fruits. For us, *first fruits* means gross income. Taxes and other deductions are so different across locales that God cannot have meant it differently for one place than for another, in our view. Further, we view this as a minimum that we are supposed to increase through sacrificial giving, which of course is unique to a family. That tithe (or more) is meant to be used for works that further Christ's message on earth; hence we do not include worthy philanthropies in that ten percent figure, although we do give to them. Finally, for us, that ten percent is not entirely pledged to our local church, although this congregation is the primary recipient of our tithe.

Today, we immediately deposit fifteen percent in a giving account for every dollar earned. We have found that if you develop good habits with small amounts it is much easier to sacrifice when the amounts get big. It also helps to remember that it all has been entrusted to us by God, and you cannot out-give the Lord; of that we are truly convinced. We give to three or four churches, the Presbyterian Seminary, and some missions that are important to us. About five percent of our funds are given to other good philanthropic stewards like Children's Theater, Fletcher School, St. Jude, etc. Our boys pick a charity that they wish to give to each year, and we make a donation in their name to encourage future giving.

As my wife and I have been financially blessed and retired debt, we have used this as an opportunity to increase our giving. Our next goal is to give twenty percent of our income, and I can't say that we will stop there. When I look back at how much we have given, I realize that it has been sacrificial—we still work hard to pay a mortgage and private school tuition for our boys' special educational needs. And yet when I realize that we truly have no unmet needs and consider the lifestyle that our family leads, I am convicted not to be too proud of our past giving and consider that we are not as sacrificial as we could be.